Source File Management
with SCCS

Source File Management with SCCS

Israel Silverberg

Uniware (Israel) Ltd.
Karmiel, Israel

Prentice Hall, Englewood Cliffs, New Jersey 07632

Library of Congress Cataloging-in-Publication Data

Silverberg, Israel.
    Source file management with SCCS / Israel Silverberg.
        p.   cm.
    Includes bibliographical references and index.
    ISBN 0-13-829771-1
    1. File organization (Computer science) 2. UNIX SCCS. 3. UNIX
(Computer operating system)   I. Title.
QA76.9.F5S55 1992
005.74--dc20   91-7326
                                                        CIP

Editorial/production supervision and interior design: *Harriet Tellem*
Cover design: *Lundgren Graphics*
Cover photo: *Westlight*
Prepress buyers: *Mary Elizabeth McCartney/Kelly Behr*
Manufacturing buyer: *Susan Brunke*
Acquisitions editor: *Gregory G. Doench*
Editorial assistant: *Joan Magrabi*

The publisher offers discounts on this book when ordered in bulk quantities. For more information, write:

Special Sales/Professional Marketing
Prentice-Hall, Inc.
Professional & Technical Reference Division
Englewood Cliffs, New Jersey 07632

UNIX is a registered trademark of UNIX System Laboratories, Inc. in the USA and other countries.

The author and publisher of this book have used their best efforts in preparing this book. These efforts include research, development, and testing of the theories and programs to determine their effectiveness. The author and publisher make no warranty of any kind, expressed or implied, with regard to these programs or the documentation contained in the book. The author and publisher shall not be liable in any event for incidental or consequential damages in connection with, or arising out of, the furnishing, performance, or use of these programs.

Printed in the United States of America

10 9 8 7 6 5 4 3 2

ISBN 0-13-829771-1

Prentice-Hall International (UK) Limited, *London*
Prentice-Hall of Australia Pty. Limited, *Sydney*
Prentice-Hall Canada Inc., *Toronto*
Prentice-Hall Hispanoamericana, S.A., *Mexico*
Prentice-Hall of India Private Limited, *New Delhi*
Prentice-Hall of Japan, Inc., *Tokyo*
Simon & Schuster Asia Pte. Ltd., *Singapore*
Editora Prentice-Hall do Brasil, Ltda., *Rio de Janeiro*

*In memory of my mother and father,
may they rest in peace.*

Contents

Chapter 6   Updating the SCCS File: The "delta" Command   65

Chapter 7   SCCS File Maintenance   73

Chapter 12   A Look at the Management Side   138

Preface

One of the anomalies of software development is that source file management becomes a concern only when there is a problem. Rarely does an organization tackle this issue as a preventive measure before the first crisis.

Like most programmers, in the early years of my computer career, I was too busy learning about programming and system design to be concerned about source file management. Only when I accepted a job as Manager of Quality Control for a savings and loan association did I become aware of the special problems of software management. This was in the mid 1970s. In those days, we still had decks of cards and changes were made with "delta decks." Source file management was accomplished by keeping all of the changes in a filing cabinet instead of a drawer in a programmer's desk. The computers have changed and the media of storage has changed, but the "filing cabinet" approach to source file management has remained intact.

My first attempt to go beyond the "filing cabinet" approach occurred several years ago when I was manager of a development team for a computer systems manufacturer. The problem was that we had as many different versions of the UNIX kernel as there were models of computers. To bring order to this chaos, a special project was created, which became known as the "Great Convergence Project."

It was that project that started me thinking about the software life cycle and source file management in a different light. The traditional concept of the software life cycle divides the world between a development cycle and a repetitive maintenance cycle. The software life cycle is often shown as a pie chart with the percentage taken by each phase (requirements definition, design, implementation, checkout, maintenance). But if you take that pie chart and eliminate maintenance as a piece of the pie, the software life cycle becomes a wheel that keeps turning through the phases of requirements definition, design, coding, and testing. The concept of maintenance therefore changes as we deal with a constantly evolving product in a constantly changing environment; the only difference between development and maintenance is the starting point. With new product development, we start with a clean slate; in the case of maintenance, we have an existing software base that is to be modified.

But do we start with a clean slate when developing a new product? How many experienced programmers write a new program from scratch? When it comes to programming, don't we usually take an old block and reshape it a bit to fit into the new structure? To fill this role, the source file management system has to take on a new dimension. The "file cabinet" has to be changed into a "library," a library of source files that can be checked out and returned with any necessary changes.

Building, maintaining, and using a source file library within the System V UNIX environment is the topic of this book. The requirements for a source library are defined in Chapter 1. The basic set of tools to create and to maintain this library constitute the UNIX Source Code Control System (SCCS). These tools are described in Chapters 2 through 9. In Chapters 10, 11, and 12, the topic switches from how SCCS works to how to put SCCS to work. While this book is based on UNIX System V SCCS, the principles and most of the discussion are applicable to other versions of UNIX.

Since this book is meant to be a practical guide to the understanding and use of SCCS, I felt that it was imperative to include the source to shell scripts (Appendixes D and F) and to an SCCS interface program (Appendix E). These source files are all that is needed to implement a basic source file maintenance system. While every effort has been made to make sure the source files are bug free, it is possible that a few of those little monsters are still hiding in the code. Also, it should be noted that this book was written on the premise that the reader has a basic knowledge of UNIX, shell programming, and 'C' programming. Thus, any discussion of the source files relates to the function and not to the technique.

I want to give special thanks to my wife, Haya, for her work in proofreading and correcting the manuscript. Being an English teacher, and not a programmer, she corrected and recorrected the text of the book. This left me free to concentrate on the content.

As every writer knows, from manuscript to book involves many people and a lot of work. Thanks to Greg Doench, my editor; Harriet Tellem, production editor; and Bill Thomas, copy editor; for their work in bringing this book to life. I also want to thank Joan Magrabi, editorial assistant; for helping solve many problems both small and large. Thanks also goes to the many people whose names I do not know, including the reviewers of this book and other staff members of Prentice Hall, for making the publication of this work possible.

Israel Silverberg
Karmiel, Israel

Ordering Information

The example programs in this book are available in computer-readable form. For ordering information write to:

Uniware (Israel) Ltd.
P.O. Box 11151
Karmiel 20100 Israel

Text Conventions

Throughout this text, the following conventions will be used to illustrate UNIX commands.

- In example statements, any input that must be entered will be in **boldface**.
- Words that are enclosed by **braces, { }**, are command-line parameters and are to be replaced with the appropriate text.
- The presence of **brackets, [ ]**, indicates that the enclosed text is optional. Multiple options are separated by a **vertical bar, |**.
- **Ellipses (. . .)** indicate that the preceding option may be repeated.
- Text enclosed in 〈 〉 indicates variables whose content is determined by the command being executed.
- The Bourne shell will be used for all examples (C shell users should have no problems making the appropriate changes). The beginning of a shell command line is indicated by a **$**.
- The C programs have been compiled and tested under System V/386, Release 3.

CHAPTER 1

Why Source File Management

1.1 Definition of a Source File

To maintain a degree of clarity within any work, there must be a common understanding of certain terms. In a field such as computers, in which old terminology continuously takes on new meanings, the definition of even the most common terms is very difficult. Therefore, to ensure clarity, the following definitions of basic terminology are used in this book. As the need arises, additional terminology related to specific areas of source file management will be defined.

The files that concern us in this book are **source files**, a common term used to describe *dynamic application text files*. To define a dynamic application text file, we must first define **text files**. These are files that contain primarily alphanumeric characters, including punctuation, but they may also contain special characters used to control printing. These files are usually created and modified through the use of a text editor or word processor.

An **application text file** is a text file created and modified by a user for an application, as opposed to special system files, such as /etc/passwd. When **application text files** reach a point where modifications cease, they then become **static files**. Such files may include correspondence, books, and magazine articles. In the process of preparing a letter, we may go through several revisions. However, once the letter is finished and mailed, the text file will probably never be changed. In this sense, it has become a **static application text file**.

Some **application text files** continue to undergo periodic cycles of modifications such that there are different versions of the file. This type of file we shall call a **dynamic application text file**. As these files are often sources for programs, they are commonly referred to as **source files**. Source files, however, are not limited to programs; they can also include documentation files.

Since there may be multiple versions of a source file, we need to define the terms used to describe the relationship between different versions. The original source file will be called the **parent source file**, and the modified source file, the **child source file**. The normal pattern is for a parent source file to have only one child source file. If a parent source file has more than one child source file, then the additional child source files will be called **branches**. Thus, as a source file changes it has many descendants, which will be referred to as the **progeny**.

Rarely does a source file exist in isolation. Usually, several source files are combined through the use of various tools to form a **product**, sometimes called a system, a software package, or an application. For example, a product can be a general ledger accounting package or it could be a reference manual. Just like the source files that compose the product, a product has a lineage in which each parent normally has one child. However, just like a source file, it too can have branches.

1.2 What Makes Source Files Dynamic

For the purposes of illustration, we will consider a software system and the associated documentation. This package will be called the *Ultimate Editor*. According to the design specifications, it is the editor that will outdo every other editor.

After many years of work, the *Ultimate Editor* has been finished and is released upon the world. After all this work, we say it is **done**; it is **completed**. But is it? Can we really just archive all the files and be done with it? Time passes, additional requirements are put forth, the computer environment has changed, and a few undetected bugs have come out of hiding. It is now necessary to start development for another release, and the cycle must begin again, except that the source code and documentation from the last release are used as the starting point.

This modification process will repeat itself again and again throughout the life of a product. For, in reality, the product is never done, never finally completed, until it is no longer used. It is this process of continual change that gives source files their identity as dynamic application text files.

1.3 The Need to Manage Change

Since the beginning of computers, software managers have had to cope with the problem of the continual changes in software that lead to what we will call *software entropy* or, as it is better known, "utter chaos." The degree of software entropy is equal to the number of changes made to a source file times the number of branches. Two examples will show how quickly software entropy can multiply when there is no management of changes to source files.

In company A, the customers are the company's departments (for example, accounting, marketing, and manufacturing). In company A, source files usually have a sequential lineage (version 3 is based on version 2, which is based on version 1). Software entropy in this environment takes the form of loss of progeny control such that version 3 of a particular source file is not based on version 2, but on version 1. An error like this can occur when several teams share parts of a common source file. Team A creates version 2 of a source file by modifying version 1. Not knowing that team A made any changes, team B modifies version 1, creating another new version. Under these conditions, which version will be the parent to the next generation? (In Chapter 10, we shall show how we can protect against this kind of error.)

Company B is a service bureau or software house. For this type of company, source files may have multiple branches caused by the special application or hardware needs of different customers. Software entropy develops very quickly when each branch is under the domain of a different development team. The end result is that each branch develops a life of its own. What was once a change to a common source file is now multiplied by the number of branches. Occasionally, not all the branches are changed, or the change conflicts with other changes made to a particular branch. This kind of situation can occur even in companies that have a source file management system, because, as we shall see, source file management is more involved than just having a faithful source file librarian.

The bottom line is that everytime there is a loss of source file control it costs money. The maintenance and enhancement of source files are already expensive propositions. It does not have to be made more expensive by poor source file management.

The requirements for a source file control system are discussed next. As you study each of these requirements, think about the costs that would be incurred if there were no software controls in that area.

1.4 Requirements for a Source File Control System

As mentioned above, the management of changes to source files, whether they represent source programs or documentation, is more than just managing the archives of different versions. For if preserving a historical copy were the only issue, a source file control system would have two requirements: the ability to save new versions and the ability to retrieve a previous version. But, as can be seen from the following list of requirements, source file management is a multifaceted issue.

1.4.1 Ability to Retrieve any Previous Version

The most important version of a source file is the parent to the next generation of a source file. To understand this requirement, let's review the difference between a dynamic text file and a static text file.

During the development phase (for example, the different drafts of a letter or the different drafts of a program), a text file may have many drafts. Once the development phase is finished, the text file can be archived. If the text file is a static text file, this is the end of the road. For a source file, the *archived version* becomes the basis for future generations.

An archive copy of a source file is not to be confused with copies of the file captured in periodic file backups. Backups are created to protect against the loss of a file due to hardware failure or operator error. Archiving source files is done with the intent of preserving copies of each generation.

1.4.2 Ability to Rebuild a Previous Version

Rebuilding a product from a previous version of the source files requires more than just being able to retrieve the source files for that version. It means that the final product, whether it be an executable file or a printed page, be identical to the product that was originally built from the source files. To fulfill this requirement, the same "build environment," which may include compilers, preprocessors, or text formatters, has to be recreated. In other words, the tools used to build a particular version of the product and the process for building the product are just as important as the source files for a product. This means that the exact sequence of the build process, including all options passed to the tools, must be documented. After all, a different version of the product can be built by changing the tools or build process with no changes to any of the constituent source files.

1.4.3 Ability to Control Progeny

Let's say that work on version 3 of the *Ultimate Editor* is about to begin. Unless otherwise planned, version 3 must be a direct descendant of version 2 and not of some other version, such as version 1. This is a simple illustration of progeny control, or having control over the descendants of a source file. While the first requirement for a source file management system allows us to retrieve any archived version, it does not require any knowledge of its heritage. Yet, without knowledge of the heritage of each version, we do not have control over the changes made to the source file.

Another aspect of progeny control is the ability to lock out any version from use in the creation of future descendants. Without this capability, it would be possible to create descendants from versions of a source file that are no longer viable. The use of this lockout capability is particularly important when branches are created for custom versions.

1.4.4 Ability to Control Access

Whether it is to prevent unauthorized changes or to prevent theft, it is important to limit access to source files. This is a very touchy area and will generate a considerable degree of heat, the intensity of which will depend on how strictly access is controlled. For the purposes of this work, the degree of access is not an important issue. What is important is that it must be dealt with, and the means must be provided to implement appropriate levels of security.

1.4.5 Edit Check-out Control

Except for the creation of a new branch, each version should only have one descendant. Prevention of the accidental creation of multiple descendants to a single parent is a necessity. It is also important to know who is currently in the process of creating a new descendant. This little bit of information can save a lot of running from desk to desk, asking who has the source file checked out for changes.

1.4.6 Convenient Access to Archived Source Files

The obvious reason for providing convenient access to source files is the cost of hours lost while the development team idly waits for source files to be retrieved from the archives. If it takes too long to get an official version of the last release, it is very tempting to start work using any version that happens to be available. A developer, using a bootlegged version, will assure her or his manager that it is identical to the official one. This gambit does not always pay off and, more often than not, results in many hours spent tracking down bugs that had been previously fixed. Murphy should have discovered this human weakness and developed a law that says that the hours spent making modifications to a source file are directly proportional to the hours spent tracking down the bugs that had been eradicated in the official version. Providing convenient access to source files minimizes losses due to these errors.

1.4.7 Minimal On-line Storage Requirements

This requirement presupposes that the system configuration provides on-line access to a source file library. While it is true that the cost of mass storage is getting cheaper, disk space still has a finite limit. The problem becomes how to achieve minimal access time and still keep on-line storage requirements to a minimum. The solution is to find the balance point between the value of minimal access time and the cost of disk space.

1.4.8 Minimal Cost for Implementation and Support

A major reason for establishing a source file control system is to avoid loss of money, time, and effort. As such, a source file control system is an insurance policy purchased for protection against these losses. Like an insurance policy, whether the source file control system is a manual system or highly automated, it costs money, time, and effort to establish and maintain it. However, these costs are far less than the cost of having no control. The objective is to provide the appropriate level of protection at a minimal cost. Sometimes, this involves trade-offs between the desired objective and cost of achieving that objective. For example, how much source file security is needed can range from no security to comprehensive access control with complete logging of every access to a source file. While the cost for providing different levels of file security can be determined, the cost of not having sufficient file security is harder to fix. Thus, choosing an appropriate level of security is a difficult decision. As in insurance, the question is how big a policy is needed.

1.4.9 Acceptance by the People Who Use It

Ultimately, any source control system will work only if the users accept it. Fulfillment of this requirement is not a simple task, for it involves the design of the system, the perception of the users (who prefer minimal controls), and the attitude of management. After setting the stage with a short review about the traditional manual approach to source control, the remainder of the book will turn to a review of SCCS and how to build a user-friendly source control system.

1.5 The Process of Source File Management

Over the years, many different models have been proposed for software development. In each of these models, someone was responsible for caring for source files. This responsibility ranged from the team librarian in the chief programmer teams concept[1] to the configuration management group in the concept described by Glass.[2] As there are many management methods, the term **source administrator** will be used as a general term to describe the person or group having source file management responsibilities. Although the need for source file management is always mentioned, little has been said about the actual process of source file management. As we shall see, who does it is secondary to what has to be done. To understand this process, a traditional manual system will be described. Later, we shall look at how UNIX tools can automate this manual system.

1.5.1 Traditional Manual System

Like any system, the manual source control system depends on the users following a set of rules. The following are five rules that exemplify a typical manual system.

Rule 1: All source files pertaining to a product, with no extraneous files, must be given to the source administrator.

How does the source administrator know if he or she has received the correct set of files? Have all the source files required to build the product been provided? Have all the work files and other junk files been removed? Unfortunately, trying to determine which files are real and which files are junk wastes a lot of time. The only sure way is to compare the list of given files against an authorized list of files.

> **Rule 2:** A complete set of instructions must be provided to the source administrator for building the product from the source files provided.

As anyone who has tried to reproduce the building of a product knows, exact and detailed instructions are necessary. Not only must these instructions specify the procedures to follow for building a product, but they must also specify all the tools used in building the product and their version numbers.

> **Rule 3:** The product as built by the software development team must be given to the source administrator.

Rules 1, 2, and 3 are part of a formula that says that *source files + build instructions = a product*. If the source files are correct, the build instructions are correct, and the product provided is correct, then the source administrator should be able to build a product that is the same as the product provided to him or her. If the two products match, then we know that the source files are correct and that the instructions for creating the product are correct. But we cannot know if junk files were included among the source files given to a source administrator unless the names were verified against an approved list of names of source files for that version of the product.

> **Rule 4:** Only those who have proper authorization can request copies of source files or submit new versions of a source file.

Normally, this refers to the development team leader. Of course, exceptions to this rule require appropriate management approval.

> **Rule 5:** The development team leader is responsible for ensuring that several people do not make simultaneous changes to a source file.

Rarely is this rule an issue with small development teams. However, when multiple teams use the same set of source files, the probability of two people working on the same source file increases dramatically. For example, a C compiler is being developed for multiple machines and each machine has its own development team. Under these circumstances, a person wishing to make a change to a source file must first clear it with the team leader.

With the above five rules, we have simulated how most organizations handle source file management. How does this manual system comply with the requirements for a source file control system as specified in Section 1.4?

1. Source files can be maintained at either the individual level or the product level. Source file management at the individual level is the most common method used when there is a single customer for a product, but there is no control over the entire product. In fact, it may be very difficult to replicate the process required to build the total product (different modules may have been built with different versions of the same tool). When the history of individual source files is subsumed in the history of a product, the source files for the entire product are usually the object of source file management rather than an individual source file. However, with no control over an individual source file, it is possible for correct versions to be replaced by incorrect versions. Source files must therefore be controlled at the product level as well as at the individual level.

2. Assuming that all versions of the tools are kept and detailed build instructions do exist, it is then possible to rebuild a product at any time. While manual procedures for building a product are adequate, they are time consuming and prone to human error. It is beyond the purpose of this book to discuss the use of UNIX tools in the building of a product. However, makefiles (a rules file for the make command) and all other text files used to control the build process are subject to version control.

3. Progeny control is difficult with a manual source file control system. Even if a source administrator keeps good records of what has been submitted, there is no guarantee that release 3 of a product will be based on release 2. The only guarantee is that the last version of the source files was used to build the current product. The real problems start when a branch is created. The normal trend is that, as the number of branches increases, each branch develops an independent existence. If all branches were truly independent, there would be no problem. However, what happens to the change that applies to all the branches? Since there is no longer a common base, the same change must be made to each branch. This lack of progeny control leads to software entropy, which, in turn, leads to higher maintenance costs.

4. The limit to any system security depends on its weakest link. All a source administrator can do is to control who gets the source files (ability to read) and who can submit changes (ability to write). Once it is beyond his or her domain, the administrator has no control over what happens to the source

file. At this point, access control is in the hands of the recipient. The larger the number of potential recipients means the larger the access control problem. The normal means of handling security problems is to tighten access from the source administrator. The normal result is that unofficial versions are then obtained from prior recipients. Thus, access control at the level of a source file control system is vital to, but still only a part of, the solution to source file security.

5. While, on the surface, it sounds feasible to have the team leader be the responsible person for managing who modifies which source files, this does have a few weaknesses. First, it means that the team leader has to have a system of keeping track of who is working on what. Even if delegated to someone else on the team, it is still a manual system subject to failure due to human error. Second, when a source file is required by different teams, the coordination of changes becomes a nightmare that is often disposed of by having separate branches—source file entropy.

6. With few exceptions, when it comes to source file control, the tendency of developers is to follow the path of least resistance. When access to the official version is too difficult, the version of a source file that is most easily available becomes the one that is used to make the change, especially if it is believed to match the official version. Just remember that source file control is more of a concern to the person managing the project than it is to the person making the change.

7. Whether or not there is a savings in on-line storage requirements depends on how the source files are archived by a source administrator. If they are stored on magnetic tape, floppy disk, or any other archival media, then the conservation of disk space is not an issue. The price paid is the time it takes to make the files available to the person who is requesting permission to use a specific version. If each version of a source file is stored in its entirety on a hard disk, then the availability of source files is improved at the expense of space conservation.

8. Since a manual system is labor intensive, the cost of control is directly related to the degree of control. At some point, the cost of source control will exceed the perceived cost of any potential loss. The term *perceived cost* is used because at the time of a disaster the perceived cost is at its maximum. As time passes, the emotional energy created by a disaster dissipates, and the perceived cost of a disaster decreases accordingly. For a source control system to survive, it has to be perceived as being an integral part of the development cycle and worth the expense.

9. As was stated above, acceptance by the user is a critical key to the success of a source control system. One way of measuring acceptance is to look at the amount of time spent on enforcing compliance to the procedures for source control. Are access control procedures being followed or circumvented? Is the correct version of the sources files for a product being used or is the most accessible version being used? Can the product be built from the instructions

provided or not? How do the users view the source control system? Is it an obstacle to doing their job or is it making their job easier? More often than not, a manual system is viewed as being an obstacle.

1.5.2 Automating Source File Management

Like the cobbler and his children, software developers are often the most reluctant to use software tools to solve their own administrative problems. This does not have to be the case. The remainder of this book will discuss some solutions to source file management problems. To accomplish this task, we shall take an in-depth look at how SCCS works, and the additional tools to move SCCS from the controlling of a single module to managing systems, and we then move on to a discussion of how to implement a source control system. As part of this discussion, we shall again return to the question of who performs what tasks.

References

1. Edward Yourdon, *How to Manage Structured Programming* (New York: Yourdon, Inc., 1976), Chap. 8.
2. Robert L. Glass, *Software Reliability Guidebook* (Englewood Cliffs, N.J.: Prentice Hall, 1979), p. 187.

CHAPTER 2

Introduction to SCCS

2.1 What Is SCCS?

The name SCCS (Source Code Control System) applies to a group of UNIX programs used to control and account for changes to source files. According to an abstract written by Rochkind,[1] development on SCCS began in late 1972. The initial version was written in SNOBOL and compiled with a SPITBOL compiler on an IBM 370. In 1973, the first UNIX version was developed on a PDP 11/45. SCCS was part of the Programmer's WorkBench (a concept created by E. L. Ivie) until the release of UNIX System V. SCCS is now distributed as part of UNIX System V. While based on SCCS in UNIX Version 7, the Berkeley version (BSD SCCS) has developed along its own path. As a result, it is conceptually the same as System V SCCS, but there are variations in the commands and their syntax.

SCCS is a system consisting of a group of programs that includes basic utilities for creating and administering an SCCS file, retrieving a source file from an SCCS file, and storing a source file in an SCCS file. In addition, SCCS provides other utility programs to assist in the management of SCCS files. Table 2.1 gives a complete list of the SCCS utilities as distributed with UNIX System V. Information on the use of these utilities is provided in Chapters 4 through 9.

While the history and name tend to emphasize source code files, SCCS has been used for many kinds of source files, including documentation. Perhaps a more appropriate name would have been Version Control System. Alas, the name is what it is, and what SCCS does is version management for text files.

TABLE 2.1 SCCS COMMANDS

Utility name	Description
admin	Create and administer an SCCS file
cdc	Change commentary to delta in an SCCS file
comp	Combine several deltas into one delta
delta	Update an SCCS file with a source file
get	Retrieve a source file from an SCCS file
help	Part of UNIX Help Facility, which provides assistance for use of SCCS commands
prs	Print SCCS file control record information
rmdel	Remove a delta from an SCCS file
sact	Print current SCCS file editing activity
sccsdiff	Compare and print the differences between two deltas in an SCCS file
unget	Cancel a previous get with edit option
val	Validate an SCCS file against a specified set of arguments
vc	Version control facility that provides for keyword substitution in the text
what	Search source file or its product for SCCS ID information

2.2 Which Version of SCCS?

The information presented in this book is based on SCCS as distributed in UNIX System V, Release 3.[2-4] According to the *SCCS/PWB User's Manual*,[5] for those readers using UNIX Version 7 and having installed PWB, the majority of the information given in this book is applicable.[6] For those using UNIX System III,[7] the commands are the same as those in System V SCCS. The only major difference is that UNIX System III did not include the **vc** command. To concentrate on System V SCCS, the differences between it and BSD SCCS will not be covered in this work.

In terms of standards, this book also follows the X/OPEN Portability Guide.[8] However, the X/OPEN document does not include the **cdc**, **comp**, **sccsdiff**, and **vc** commands.

2.3 Alternatives to SCCS

Version control systems have been around for some time. However, the choices within the world of UNIX are limited. RCS (Revision Control System), developed by Walter F. Tichy of Purdue University, is an alternative that has a significant following. As of the writing of this book, RCS was available for a nominal fee. Other version control systems have been developed for UNIX, but none have reached the popularity of SCCS and RCS.

While there are significant differences between SCCS and RCS, the principles of source file management set forth in this book apply to both. So that we can concentrate on the principles of source file management, SCCS will be the only source file control system referenced in the remainder of this book.

2.4 Command Conventions

Before taking a quick tour of SCCS, the following is a short review of the SCCS command conventions. Exceptions to these conventions will be noted under the discussion of individual SCCS commands. The basic format for a UNIX command is

$ command [-x{optional variable}] {arguments}

where the **-x** refers to an option or, as it is sometimes called, a **flag**. **Options** and **arguments** constitute the two means of modifying the action of a UNIX command. Most UNIX commands can be executed without specifying any options or arguments. Thus, it is important to understand the default action of each command.

 Options always have the format of a **minus sign (-)** followed by a letter of the alphabet, called the **keyletter**. Some options may also require a variable following the keyletter. The keyletter specifies the nature of the option; for example, the -n option of the admin command says that a new SCCS file is to be created. If the option requires a variable to be given, the variable must immediately follow the keyletter and must not contain any spaces or tabs. If the variable contains spaces or tabs, the variable must be enclosed in double quotes " ", for example, delta **-y"this is an example"**.

 Arguments normally refer to file names. If the file name given is the name of a directory, then it is as if all files in the directory are specified. Most SCCS commands will automatically ignore any non-SCCS files or files without read permission. The minus sign **(-)** that stands alone is a special argument that causes the command to read the standard input for a list of file names. In this case, each line of the standard input is taken to be a file name. This form of the file name is often used in conjunction with the **find** or **ls** commands. For example, the command

$ ls s.exmpl* | get -

will retrieve all the SCCS files in the current directory beginning with the characters "s.exmpl".

2.5 A Quick Tour of SCCS

As we shall see in Chapter 3, the key to SCCS is the SCCS file, which contains the information necessary to recreate any version of a source file. To distinguish SCCS files from source files, source file names are prefixed with "s.". For example, the SCCS File name for the source file **exmpl.c** would be **s.exmpl.c**.

 For this quick tour of SCCS, we shall assume that we have a source file called **exmpl.c** to which we want to apply version control (see the Glossary for a definition of the term *version control*). The first step in this process is to create an SCCS file by using the **admin** command (see Chapter 4). For our example, the command is as follows:

$ admin -n -iexmpl.c s.exmpl.c

The above **admin** command creates a new (**-n**) SCCS file called **s.exmpl.c** and includes (**-i**) **exmpl.c** as the first delta. As we shall see in Chapter 3, SCCS tracks each version by keeping the differences (**delta**) between the parent source file and the child source file. For the initial delta, the semantics of SCCS make more sense if you think of the initial delta as having a null parent.

Since the SCCS File is a special file that should be edited only in rare circumstances (see Chapter 7), we need a way of retrieving a source file from the SCCS File. This function is performed by the **get** command (see Chapter 5). To retrieve the last change made, we enter the command

$ get s.exmpl.c

The above command creates a read-only file called **exmpl.c**. However, if we are intending to change the file, SCCS must be notified of this intent to edit the file. To do this, we would enter the command as follows:

$ get -e s.exmpl.c

The **-e** option signals SCCS to make the retrieved file writable and, through the use of a work file called a **p-file**, prevents anyone else from retrieving the same version of the file for editing. Once we have completed the changes to the source file and are ready to store the new version in the SCCS file, we use the **delta** command (see Chapter 6). The **delta** command compares the child source file against the parent source file, as defined by the **p-file**, and stores the differences in the SCCS file. To store the new version of **exmpl.c**, we would use the following command:

$ delta s.exmpl.c

While each of the above commands has many options, the basic process is always to create an SCCS file with the **admin** command, to retrieve a source file from the SCCS file with the **get** command, and to store a source file in an SCCS file with the **delta** command. Additional SCCS commands are used to maintain an SCCS file (see Chapter 7) and to extract information from an SCCS file (Chapter 8). Other miscellaneous commands are discussed in Chapter 9. In Chapters 10 through 12, these SCCS commands will be brought together, with the shell scripts provided in Appendix F. The result will be version control of a product instead of a single source file.

2.6 Error Messages and the "help" Command

As a general rule, SCCS commands display error messages in the following format:

<error message> <error code>

The <error message> phrase can be in either one of the two following formats:

<message text>

or

ERROR <name of file being processed>: <message text>

The <error code> is an alphanumeric code that can be used in conjunction with the **help** command to obtain more information regarding the error. The following are examples of SCCS error messages:

No id keywords (cm7)
ERROR [s.junk.c]: 's.junk.c' nonexistent (ut4)

While the **help** command under UNIX System V constitutes a complete help facility, it is still compatible with the version of the command that was strictly an SCCS utility. The primary purpose of the **help** command is to provide more information about SCCS errors. In addition, it can be used to show the syntax for any SCCS command. For the purposes of SCCS, the format of the command is as follows:

$ help [{error code} | {SCCS command}] . . .

For example, if more information is needed about the ut4 error code (see above example of error messages), the command

$ help ut4

produces

ut4:
" '. . .' nonexistent"
The file does not exist. Check for typos.

By the same token, the syntax for the SCCS command "rmdel" can be obtain by the following:

$ help rmdel

rmdel:
rmdel -rSID file . . .

Note that the above does not describe all the features of the expanded version of the **help** command. For more information, see the *UNIX System V User's Reference Manual*.[9]

References

1. Marc J. Rochkind, *The Source Code Control System* (Original Working Paper, n.p., n.d.), p. 1.
2. AT&T, *UNIX System V: User's Reference Manual* (Englewood Cliffs, N.J.: Prentice Hall, 1987).
3. AT&T, *UNIX System V: Programmer's Reference Manual* (Englewood Cliffs, N.J.: Prentice Hall, 1987).
4. AT&T, *UNIX System V: Programmer's Guide* (Englewood Cliffs, N.J.: Prentice Hall, 1987).
5. L. E. Bonanni and A. L. Glasser, *SCCS/PWB User's Manual* (n.p.: Bell Telephone Laboratories, Inc., 1977).
6. The following commands were not available with UNIX Version 7: **sact**, **unget**, **val**, and **vc**. Also, the Version 7 **prt** command is less flexible than the **prs** command. The Version 7 **chghist** performs the same function as the **cdc** command, but with a slightly different syntax. Finally, Version 7 SCCS has fewer flags in the Flag Table.
7. L. E. Bonanni and C. A. Salemi, *Source Code Control System User's Guide* (n.p.: Bell Telephone Laboratories, Inc., 1980).
8. X/Open Company Ltd., *X/OPEN Portability Guide, Volume 1: XSI Commands and Utilities* (Englewood Cliffs, N.J.: Prentice Hall, 1989).
9. AT&T, *UNIX System V: User's Reference Manual*, p. 127.

CHAPTER 3

The SCCS File

3.1 The Importance of the SCCS File

The heart of SCCS is the SCCS file. To gain an understanding of an SCCS file, we must first look at the different ways that the various versions of a source file can be tracked, culminating in a discussion of the delta file concept. From this concept, we shall learn that an SCCS file is the merger of all the delta files into a single file. A section follows on the naming of deltas and the concept of progeny control in an SCCS file. Finally, there is a discussion of the SCCS file structure and control records. As we shall see in subsequent chapters, the SCCS commands do nothing more than create, maintain, and provide reports about this file.

3.2 Keeping Track of Change

With the exception of possible changes to tools or build instructions, the release of a new version of a product involves making changes to one or more source files. As discussed in Chapter 1, one requirement for a source file control system is that the system have the ability to track different versions of a source file. Not only do these different versions of the source files have to be tracked, but we also need to have convenient access to them. These goals can be fulfilled by requiring that all versions of the source files for a product be maintained on readily accessible media, such as a fixed disk. The issue then is how to keep the disk space requirements to a minimum. Let's start first by reviewing the traditional ways of organizing the disk file structure for version tracking.

3.2.1 Keeping Copies of Each Version

A simple, traditional way to track different versions of a source file is to keep a complete copy of each version. This can be accomplished at either the product level or at the individual source file level.

When source files are tracked at the product level, the version of the source file is linked to the version of the product. Under this schema, the version of an individual source file is considered to be the same version as that of the product. It makes no difference whether or not a source file actually changed. We can illustrate this by using the UNIX file structure in which we could have a new top-level directory for each version of the product. By having multiple source trees, the individual source file names do not change, making retrieval a simple matter of copying the entire source tree. Figure 3.1 illustrates tracking at the product level.

Alternatively, source files can be tracked individually. When tracked individually, each source file has its own version history independent of the product. To implement this approach under UNIX, we need only create one source tree with all versions of a source file in the same directory. As illustrated in Figure 3.2, the source file names have to change in order to separate the different versions of a source file. Thus, filea-1.c is version 1 of filea.c and fileb-2.c is version 2 of

```
        (version 1)                      (version 2)
         prod-01.src                      prod-02.src
   ┌─────────┼─────────┐            ┌─────────┼─────────┐
dir-a.src dir-b.src dir-c.src    dir-a.src dir-b.src dir-c.src
   │         │         │            │         │         │
filea.c   filec.c   filee.c      filea.c   filec.c   filee.c
fileb.c   filed.c   filef.c      fileb.c   filed.c   filef.c
```

Figure 3.1 Version Tracking at the Product Level

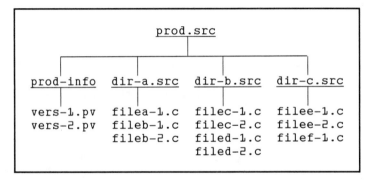

```
                        prod.src
        ┌───────────┬───────────┬───────────┐
    prod-info   dir-a.src   dir-b.src   dir-c.src
        │           │           │           │
    vers-1.pv   filea-1.c   filec-1.c   filee-1.c
    vers-2.pv   fileb-1.c   filec-2.c   filee-2.c
                fileb-2.c   filed-1.c   filef-1.c
                            filed-2.c
```

Figure 3.2 Version Tracking at the Source File Level

fileb.c. Since the source files that constitute any particular version of a product are no longer grouped together, we need to select the correct version of each source file to build any particular version of a product.

Both approaches have drawbacks. When tracked at the product level, we save an entire copy of a product even if only one file changed. In addition to wasting disk space, this approach only provides progeny control at the product level and not at the source file level. On the other hand, tracking at the source file level makes it difficult to determine which source file versions were used to build a particular version of a product. As we shall discuss in Chapter 10, the solution is to create a **product version file**. It is this product version file that will tell us which versions of the source file went into building each version of the product. In Figure 3.2, the product version file is kept in its own directory and is called vers-1.pv for version 1 of the product, vers-2.pv for version 2 of the product, and so on.

If we were to take a survey, we would probably find that most organizations attempt to manage their source files using sundry variations of the above schemata. Let's see how well these schemata comply with the requirements set forth in Chapter 1.

1. *Progeny control:* The comments made in Chapter 1 regarding progeny control under a manual system can easily be illustrated. Using Figure 3.2, let's assume that fileb-2.c is the descendant of fileb-1.c. If a fileb-3.c is added to the directory, there is no guarantee that it is a descendant of fileb-2.c. It could just as easily be a descendant of fileb-1.c. Outside of knowing the order in which the files were created, we know nothing about the history of a file. Unless, of course, the authors of the source file are all of the diligent variety who, even under extreme pressure for time, adequately document their work!

   For another variation of the above problem, let's say that Figure 3.2 represents the source tree for a compiler on microprocessor x1. A new microprocessor called the y30 has been introduced to the market and it has been decided to port the compiler to it. The resulting source control system might then look like Figure 3.3. How much do we really know about the relationship of filef-2.c for microprocessor x1 and filef-2.c for microprocessor y30? Based on the information shown, we cannot be absolutely sure about the nature of the relationship. Version 1 of the y30 files could be derived from either version

```
      (microprocessor x1)                        (microprocessor y30)
          prod-x1.src                                 prod-y30.src
  ┌──────────┼──────────┐              ┌──────────┼──────────┐
dir-a.src dir-b.src dir-c.src      dir-a.src dir-b.src dir-c.src
  │          │          │              │          │          │
filea-1.c filec-1.c filee-1.c      filea-1.c filec-1.c filee-1.c
filea-2.c filec-2.c filee-2.c      filea-2.c filec-2.c filee-2.c
fileb-1.c filed-1.c filef-1.c      fileb-1.c filed-1.c filef-1.c
fileb-2.c filed-2.c filef-2.c      fileb-2.c filed-2.c filef-2.c
```

Figure 3.3   Version Tracking for Different Branches

1 or version 2 of the equivalent x1 file. If a new feature has to be added to
the compiler, then the source trees have to be changed and tested as if they
were not related. Not only does this extra work increase the amount of
resources required to implement the new feature, but it also increases the
risk of having slightly different products.

2. *Edit check-out control:* Imagine that programmer A is in the process of making
   a modification to filed-2.c and, not knowing of programmer A's work, programmer B also decides to change filed-2.c. Once again, this manual source
   file control system does not provide any means of protecting the integrity of
   the source files. It is altogether possible for programmer A to finish his or
   her work and save the updated version as filed-3.c. Programmer B completes
   his or her work and, not remembering that he or she started with filed-2.c,
   saves his or her update as filed-4.c. It does not take a great deal of imagination
   to see the amount of chaos that this kind of error can cause.

3. *Space utilization:* For a small product with few source files and few changes,
   the amount of disk space needed for keeping each version as a complete
   source file would be wasteful but would not represent a major cost issue. It
   is wasteful in the sense that only a small percentage of the total space allocated
   between various versions of a source file is because of differences in text. It
   would make for an interesting study, but experience has shown that less than
   10% of the lines are affected for a majority of the changes made to a source
   file. If this is the case, then by keeping multiple versions of the same file, we
   are keeping many copies of duplicate text. When the number of source files
   increases or the number of changes increases, the amount of space consumed
   because of duplicate text becomes much more significant and so does the
   corresponding costs.

4. *Security of source files:* Under the above schemata, security is limited to the
   file permissions provided by UNIX. Given this situation, the two issues are
   (1) who has read permission and (2) who has write permission. Normally,
   the number of people who have read permission is much larger than those
   who have write permission. For instance, customer support personnel must
   be able to read the source to answer questions, but they would not be able
   to make changes.

   However, implementing this distinction gets to be a bit of a problem.
   Unless everybody with access to the system is to have access to the source
   files, read access to "others" must be denied. Since there can only be one
   "owner" of the source file (presumably the source administrator), the "group"
   permission bears the burden of defining those who have read permission. The
   same logic can be applied to write permission, and, once again, the "group"
   permission comes up as the winner. But, since a file can only have one group
   assigned, we are forced to bundle the read group with the write group, which
   is not what we wanted. How can this problem be resolved? If source files are
   managed using a variation of one of the above schemata, then the traditional
   answer has been to deny group write permission and make the source administrator responsible for all changes. As we shall see in Chapter 10, there
   is another solution.

Now that we know more about the problems we need to solve, we can move on to the solutions. The following section shows how the delta file concept reduces the amount of space wasted because of duplication. From there we move on to solving the question of progeny control, and then to SCCS solutions for joint edit control, and delta control.

3.2.2 The Delta File Concept

How can we reduce the amount of space taken by keeping all these separate versions of source files? One answer is to keep only the original version as a complete file. Instead of saving a complete copy of a revised version of a source file, only the differences between the original file and the revised version will be saved. This special file is called a **delta** file.

As an illustration of a delta file, let Figure 3.4 be the original source file and Figure 3.5 be the revised source file. The difference between the two figures is the change in line 2 and the addition of line 5. Assuming that these source files were saved in files called exmpl-1.t and exmpl-2.t, respectively, the command

$ diff -e exmpl-1.t exmpl-2.t > exmpl-2.d

will produce the delta file exmpl-2.d (the suffix "**.d**" will be used to identify a delta file) as shown in Figure 3.6.

To rebuild exmpl-2.t from exmpl-1.t, we have to combine the delta, exmpl-2.d with exmpl-1.t. As we can see from Figure 3.6, the delta file contains the necessary add, change, and delete commands that **ed** needs to re-create the revised version of the source file from the original version. The **ed** command line used to do this is as follows:

$ (cat exmpl-2.d; echo '1,$p') | ed exmpl-1.t > exmpl-2.t

```
This is line 1; revision 0.
This is line 2; revision 0.
This is line 3; revision 0.
This is line 4; revision 0.
```

Figure 3.4   Original Source File

```
This is line 1; revision 0.
This is line 2; revision 1.
This is line 3; revision 0.
This is line 4; revision 0.
This is line 5; revision 1.
```

Figure 3.5   Revised Source File

```
4a
This is line 5; revision 1.
.
2c
This is line 2; revision 1.
.
```

Figure 3.6   Delta File Created by diff Command

When there are many versions of a source file, each version, or child source file, is the result of changes from the previous version, the parent source file. The difference between a child source file and its parent is defined by a delta file. Of course, the term parent source file is a relative term, because the parent source file is a child source file to its parent. For each generation, the difference is defined by a delta file. Creation of the desired child source file is the result of combining all the delta files to the initial parent source file.

For example, if there was a version 3 of the above file called **exmpl-3.t**, it would have a corresponding delta file called **exmpl-3.d**. However, the command

```
$ (cat exmpl-3.d; echo '1,$p') | ed exmpl-1.t > exmpl-3.t
```

would not produce the correct result. Why? Because **exmpl-3.t** was based on **exmpl-2.t**. Therefore, the delta file exmpl-3.d only contains the differences between exmpl-2.t and exmpl-3.t. To re-create exmpl-3.t, the correct series of commands is

```
$ (cat exmpl-2.d; echo '1,$p') | ed exmpl-1.t > temp-2.t
$ (cat exmpl-3.d; echo '1,$p') | ed temp-2.t > exmpl-3.t
$ rm temp-2.t
```

In other words, you start with the initial file and add all the deltas required to get to the desired version of the source file. This process of sequentially applying separate delta files was the concept behind the first version control systems. By first version control systems, we are talking about the days of punched cards when "delta decks" were used to update the main "program deck."

In the punched card days, the delta deck was directly created by the programmer. With the advent of on-line editing of source files, the parent source file is now directly modified to create the child source file. Once the changes are finished, the next generation of delta file needs to be generated by comparing the child source file to the parent source file. However, since only delta files are retained, a copy of the parent does not exist and so must be re-created. In the example shown above, the steps are as follows:

```
$ (cat exmpl-2.d; echo '1,$p') | ed exmpl-1.t > temp-2.t
$ (cat exmpl-3.d; echo '1,$p') | ed temp-2.t > temp-3.t
$ diff -e temp-3.t exmpl-4.t > exmpl-4.d
$ rm -f temp* exmpl-4.t
```

If we were to look at the source tree that results from using the delta file concept, Figure 3.2 would look like Figure 3.7.

As can be seen from the above, if most changes are relatively small in comparison to the original source file, the delta file concept will result in a considerable savings in disk space. However, except for improvements in space utilization, the other problems discussed in the previous section still exist. As we shall see in the next section, SCCS is an enhanced form of the delta file concept that resolves these problems.

It should noted that sequentially adding deltas represents one approach to

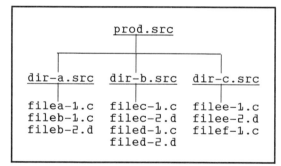

Figure 3.7 Version Tracking
Using Delta Files

version tracking. RCS uses the reverse approach by keeping a complete copy of the current source file and reverse deltas to go back to previous versions. While this approach improves the speed of access to the current version, it takes considerably more disk space to maintain a file that has multiple branches. This is the result of having to maintain a complete source file for every branch.

3.3 The SCCS File Concept

The basic concept behind SCCS is to combine all the delta files for one original source file into one file, the SCCS file. Remember, a delta file consists of nothing more than the changes between two versions of a source file along with the necessary edit commands. By linking each edit command to a particular delta, it becomes possible to merge all the deltas. How this is done will be explained in Section 3.5.6.

Since the SCCS file is a special type of file, there needs to be a means of easily distinguishing it from other files. This is accomplished by prefixing all SCCS files with the characters "**s.**". Thus, the SCCS file for the source file **exmpl.t** would be **s.exmpl.t**. If Figure 3.7 were converted into SCCS files, the result would be as shown in Figure 3.8. Notice that all the delta files have disappeared, since they are now a part of the SCCS file.

However, if the SCCS file was just a collection of the delta files into one file, the **ar** (archive) command could be used instead of having an entire set of new commands. What makes the SCCS file different is that it also keeps track of the information necessary to build a source file from a given delta using a process similar to, but considerably more elegant than, the additive process described

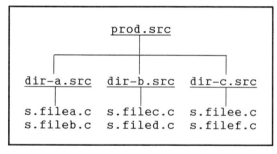

Figure 3.8 Version Tracking
Using SCCS Files

above. In addition, other historical information is kept for each delta. While this would be sufficient to handle the tracking of a simple linear series of revisions to source files, the SCCS file also provides the necessary control information to manage more complex tracking of deltas to source files. Plus, there are control records for security, control of editing, and other information. But before discussing the exact format of the SCCS file, we need to understand how SCCS names deltas.

3.4 The SCCS Method of Naming Deltas

From the above, we can see that SCCS is a system based on deltas. Also, there is a direct link between the delta and the version of the source file. For example, version 2 of the source file is equal to the sum of the delta for version 1 plus the delta for version 2. Thus, to retrieve a particular version of a source file, we need only identify the final delta that created the version we wish to retrieve. In the above examples, deltas were sequentially numbered. In the same manner, SCCS uses a **delta sequence number** to internally identify each delta. However, the delta sequence number only tells the order in which the delta was created. It does not provide much identifying information about a delta. To resolve this problem, SCCS externally identifies a delta by a name called the **SCCS IDentification string (SID)**. The SID is composed of four numbers in the format

<Release #>.<Level #>.<Branch #>.<Sequence #>

where the branch and sequence numbers are present only when the delta is a branch delta (see below). But what does this naming convention mean?

Without going into the details of the life cycle of software, let's just say that the release number is used to identify major releases of a source file. Since SCCS has no way of knowing the difference between major and minor versions of a source file, the release number is controlled by the user and not by SCCS. Unless it is changed at the time the SCCS file is created (see Section 4.4), the default is to set the release number 1.

The level number is used to identify each delta within a release and is under the control of SCCS. SCCS does not define a level number of 0, so the first level number will be 1. For example, the default name of the first delta would be 1.1. Ignoring the possibilities of branches for a moment, a series of deltas could be numbered as shown in Figure 3.9.

Branching does what the word implies. At some point in the life of a source file, a special version might need to be created that is not part of the main trunk. For instance, one customer requires a special modification that is unique to his

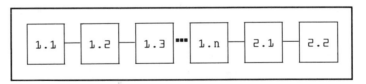

Figure 3.9   Version Numbering with No Branches

business. If branches are being supported in the SCCS file, a branch delta can be created. For example, if this branch occurred at delta 1.3, the new delta would be named 1.3.1.1. The branch number is 1 since it is the first branch from delta 1.3. The sequence number is 1 because it is the first delta in that branch. As shown in Figure 3.10, subsequent deltas on this branch would be named 1.3.1.2, 1.3.1.3, and so on.

As can be seen from Figures 3.9 and 3.10, SCCS provides the means for identifying the progeny of any delta by looking at its delta name. However, there is a limit to the system used by SCCS. If a second branch were created from version 1.3, the first delta would be named 1.3.2.1, because it is the first delta on the second branch. As with the first branch, subsequent deltas would be numbered 1.3.2.2, 1.3.2.3, and so on. This concept is illustrated in Figure 3.11.

The form of multiple branches to a single trunk delta shown in Figure 3.11 does not create a problem. However, in addition to branches from the trunk, SCCS also allows a branch to be created from a branch. The name for this new branch would be determined by incrementing the branch number and setting the sequence number to 1. For example, if, as shown in Figure 3.10, only one branch existed and a new branch was to be created from delta 1.3.1.2, the new delta name would be 1.3.2.1. The resulting delta tree is shown in Figure 3.12.

The problem is that the delta name no longer shows the exact progeny of

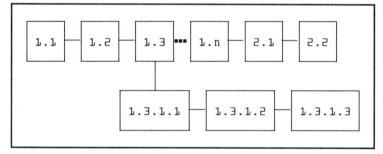

Figure 3.10   Version Numbering with One Branch

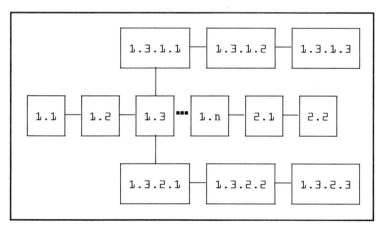

Figure 3.11   Version Numbering with Two Branches

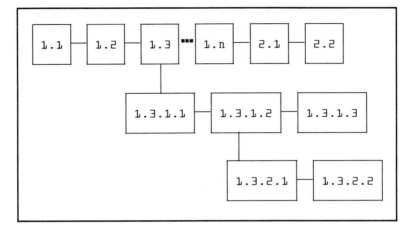

Figure 3.12   Version Numbering with Two Branches

this branch delta. For the delta name to accurately reflect its ancestry, it would have to have been named 1.3.1.2.1.1, where the branch number and sequence number become a repetitive group (the naming system used by RCS). While the name is more exact, it is also rather unmanageable. So, although some information is lost, the SID is kept to a more manageable name. Section 3.5.2 will show how the actual parentage of any branch of any delta can be identified.

3.5 SCCS File Format

From the above discussions, we know that an SCCS file is an archive of the deltas for the different versions of a source file. But it is also much more: each SCCS file is a self-contained unit that contains the deltas, delta history, control parameters, and all the other information that is maintained by SCCS. To keep track of all this information, the SCCS file is divided into six parts, which are illustrated in Figure 3.13.

The SCCS file is a mixture of text lines and SCCS control records. An **SCCS control record** always begins with an **SOH** (control-A) character as the first character in the record. Throughout this book, the **SOH** will be referred to as the **SCCS control character** and will be represented by a **@**.

Note that it is for this reason that any file that may have a **SOH** as the first character in a record *cannot* be supported by SCCS. This limitation is not common in text files, but it may appear in executable files.

Checksum
Delta table
User table
Flag table
Descriptive text
Body of source

Figure 3.13 Layout of an SCCS File

The following sections describe each part of an SCCS file. As you will see, the SCCS file contains all the information necessary for the management of a single source file. What SCCS does not provide for is the management of an entire product that consists of a group of source files. How to go from individual source file management to that of a product will be discussed later in Chapters 10 to 12.

3.5.1 SCCS File Checksum

The first line of an SCCS file is always the checksum and has the format

@hDDDDD

The **@h** identifies this as the checksum control record. The **DDDDD** is the checksum for the file in decimal. It is the sum of all the characters in the file, except for those in this line. The checksum is used to validate the integrity of the SCCS file by various SCCS commands. Any discrepancy between this line and the checksum computed by the SCCS command will result in an error, and the command will terminate.

> Note that it is because of the checksum that an SCCS file *cannot be modified by any editor or utility other than an SCCS command*. After all, the change, deletion, or insertion of only one character will change the value of the checksum. There are a few rare instances where the checksum may have to be corrected. Details on how to do emergency repair of an SCCS file and how to correct the checksum will be found in Chapter 7 on SCCS file maintenance.

3.5.2 SCCS File Delta Table

This portion of the SCCS file consists of a repetitive group of lines that describes each delta made to the SCCS file. The format of the lines for each group is as follows:

@s DDDDD/DDDDD/DDDDD
@d <type> <SID> yr/mo/da hr:mi:se <prgmr> DDDDD DDDDD
@i DDDDD . . .
@x DDDDD . . .
@g DDDDD . . .
@m <MR number>
.
.
.
@c <comments> . . .
.
.
.
@e

The **@s** line is a summary of the number of changes made by that delta and has the following format: inserted/deleted/unchanged. These counts are linked to the edit commands generated when a delta is made. Notice that the number of lines changed is not counted. The reason for this is described in the section on the SCCS file body of source.

The **@d** line gives the details regarding this delta. This line and the next three lines define how a source file is to be created from this delta. The following are definitions of the variables used in the **@d** line:

- The <**type**> of delta can either be a **D** for a normal delta or an **R** for a removed delta. The removed delta is a result of the **rmdel** command, which changes the type of delta but does not actually remove the delta information. By keeping this delta information, an audit trail of all deltas made to the SCCS file is maintained.
- The **SID** is the delta name as described in Section 3.4.
- The next two fields define the date and time of the delta. These two fields are checked by the **get** command. If, by chance, the system clock was set back between the time of the **delta** and the time of a **get**, the **get** will issue a warning message. Fixing this problem is described in Chapter 7 on SCCS file maintenance.
- The <**prgmr**> is the login name from the /etc/passwd file based on the *real user ID*, which is the **login ID**, at the time the delta was created. The distinction between real and *effective user ID* is important when delta access is controlled (see Chapter 11 for details).
- The next two numbers, shown as **DDDDD DDDDD**, define the delta sequence numbers of the current delta and its predecessor, respectively. Here is the real core of how SCCS controls the progeny of the different deltas. The deltas are sequentially numbered starting with 1. Remember, a delta file is created by taking the difference between the starting source file and the source file that is deltaed. By using the predecessor delta sequence number and the delta sequence numbers for the **@i, @x**, and **@g** records

defined below, it is possible to re-create the starting source file. In turn, the predecessor delta sequence number will define how it was created, and so on, until a null predecessor delta sequence number has been reached.

The **@i** record is an optional record and, if present, defines the delta sequence numbers of the deltas to be included to re-create the starting source file. How this option can be used will be shown below when describing the -i option of the **get** command.

The **@x** record is another optional record that, if present, defines the delta sequence numbers of the ancestor deltas to be excluded in building the starting source file. For more information, see the -x option of the **get** command.

The **@g** record is also an optional record. However, if present, it defines the delta sequence numbers to be ignored when the SCCS file is accessed for the particular SID created by the delta. Note that it is the **delta** command that creates the **@g** record and not the **get** command, as was the case with the @i and @x records.

The **@m** record is for informational purposes and contains the modification request (MR) number. If each change is tracked via some manual or automated system, the identification number of the change order, or whatever name it is called, can be logged with the associated change as the MR number. Since more then one change order may be resolved in a single delta, it is possible to have multiple **@m** records.

The **@c** is the comment line and, unless a null comment is entered, will exist for every delta. Each delta is allowed to have multiple comment records.

The **@e** record serves the function of marking the end of each delta information group.

3.5.3 SCCS File User Table

This section has the following format:

```
@u
<user login name> | <numerical group ID>
    .
    .
    .
@U
```

The purpose is to define the list of users that may add deltas to this SCCS file. Individuals are identified by the login name as defined in the /etc/passwd file. All members of the group can be given access by using the numerical group ID as defined in the /etc/group file. If no names or group IDs are listed, then anyone who has write permission in the directory is allowed to make a delta to the file. The use of this field will be discussed in more detail in Section 10.4 on SCCS file security.

3.5.4 SCCS File Flag Table

The fourth section of an SCCS file is the flag table. As can be seen from Appendix A, each flag sets a particular attribute for the SCCS file. The flags are maintained by the **admin** command and will be discussed in detail in the various sections related to the **admin** command functions (see Chapters 4 and 7). The format of each flag record is

@f <flag> <optional text>

Note that the System V documentation[1] in sccsfile(4) makes reference to a **z** flag. Ignore what the documentation says. This flag is not supported. It seems to refer to an application interface and looks for a **.FRED** file. The format for this file and how it relates to the **z** flag is absent from all the System V documentation.

3.5.5 SCCS File Descriptive Text

The fifth section contains user-defined text that can be used for comments that are not related to a specific delta. The text is bracketed by lines containing a **@t** and **@T**, so that the format of the section is

@t
<text>
.
.
.
@T

3.5.6 SCCS File Body of Source

The last section contains the actual deltas of the source file. In addition to the text lines, it contains the control lines used to insert and delete text. The format of these lines is

@I DDDDD
@D DDDDD
@E DDDDD

The **@I** or **@D** start the block of text to be inserted or deleted and the **@E** is used to terminate the block. The **DDDDD** defines the delta sequence number of the delta to which this block is connected. For example, an insert block for a delta with a delta sequence number of 2 is formatted as follows:

@I 2
<text>
.

.

.
@E 2

Thus, the **body of source** consists of delta sequence numbered blocks of inserted and deleted text. Even a change to a line of text simply requires that the old line be deleted and a new line inserted. Based on this concept of delta sequence numbered blocks of text, it is possible for deltas to be included, excluded, or ignored when a source file is created.

3.6 An Actual SCCS File

Figure 3.14 shows the SCCS file created from Figures 3.4 and 3.5. While this file is very simple, it illustrates the SCCS file concepts that we have been discussing. Any questions regarding a particular line can be answered by referring back to the section indicated in the figure.

```
@h32656
```
Checksum
(3.5.1)

```
@s 00002/00001/00003
@d D 1.2 89/01/30 18:40:01 pgmr2 2 1
@m SPR002
@c Example for Figure 3.5
@e
@s 00004/00000/00000
@d D 1.1 89/01/30 18:35:44 pgmr1 1 0
@m SPR001
@c Example for Figure 3.4
@e
```
Delta table
(3.5.2)

```
@u
pgmr1
pgmr2
@U
```
User table
(3.5.3)

```
@f b
@f n
@f q example
@f v
```
Flag table
(3.5.4)

```
@t
This is an example of an SCCS file
@T
```
Descriptive text
(3.5.5)

Figure 3.14   Sample SCCS File

```
@I 1
This is line 1; revision 0.
@D 2
This is line 2; revision 0.
@E 2
@I 2
This is line 2; revision 1.
@E 2
This is line 3; revision 0.
This is line 4; revision 0.
@I 2
This is line 5; revision 1.
@E 2
@E 1
```

Body of source
(3.5.6)

Figure 3.14   *continued*

References

1. AT&T, *UNIX System V: Programmer's Reference Manual* (Englewood Cliffs, N.J.: Prentice Hall, 1987) p. 570.

CHAPTER 4

Establishing
SCCS Files
The "admin" Command

4.1 Introduction

Before a source file can be stored in an SCCS file, the SCCS file must be created by the **admin** command. When creating the SCCS file, the **admin** command also allows for the following:

- Initial delta for a source file to be made
- User access table to be defined
- SCCS file flags to be set
- Descriptive text to be loaded

As we shall see later, except for the delta table and the body of source, the **admin** command can be used to modify all sections of the SCCS file. However, in this chapter we shall only be concerned with the initial creation of an SCCS file. Use of the **admin** command for modification of an existing SCCS file will be discussed in Chapter 7 on SCCS file maintenance.

4.2 Command Syntax

When creating an SCCS file, the format for the **admin** command is as follows:

admin [-n] [-i[{name}]] [-m{mrlist}] [-r{rel}]
[-y{comment}] [-a{login name | numerical group ID}]
[-f{flag}[{flag-val}]] [-t{text file}] {file . . .}

The following sections will explain the above syntax in more detail. Since each option is used to initialize certain portions of the SCCS file (see Chapter 3 for an explanation of the segments of an SCCS file), the following discussion is organized as follows:

- Create an SCCS file with no other options
- Modify an initial delta
- Define the user table
- Define the flag table
- Descriptive text section

4.3 Creating the Null File

A *null SCCS file* is an SCCS file with no initial delta. The format of the command used to create a null SCCS file is as follows:

admin -n {file . . .}

The **-n** option causes the **admin** command to create an SCCS with the initial delta being a null delta. The argument {**file . . .**} can either be a single file, a list of files, or a **-** (see Section 2.4 for an explanation of file naming conventions). With any of these variations, the file name must be given and it must be prefixed by an "**s.**". Thus, **s.exampl.c** is a valid SCCS file name, but **wrong.c** is not and will be rejected by **admin**.

For example, the command

$ admin -n s.exampl.c

would create an SCCS file that would look like Figure 4.1. This minimal file defines a null delta, a null user table, and an empty descriptive text segment. Notice, also, that the body of source defines an insert for a null block of text.

To protect the SCCS file from accidental changes by non-SCCS commands, an SCCS file is created with the file mode set to 444 (owner, group, and others have read permission). This file mode *must not be changed*, except under special file repair conditions as described in Section 7.4.

Having created the initial SCCS file, let's expand the command line to fill in the sections of the SCCS file with information other than the default information.

```
@h07589
@s 00000/00000/00000
@d D 1.1 89/02/01 16:10:47 pgmr1 1 0
@c date and time created 89/02/01 16:10:47 by pgmr1
@e
@u
@U
@t
@T
@I 1
@E 1
```

Figure 4.1   Example of a Null SCCS File

4.4 Modifying the Initial Delta

For the **admin** command syntax shown above, the following options relate to the modification of the initial delta to the SCCS file being created:

[-i[{name}]]	Include a source file
[-m{mrlist}]	Define modification request numbers
[-r{rel}]	Change the release number
[-y{comment}]	Change the comment

The **-i** option allows the initial delta to include lines of text into the SCCS file being created. If specified, **{name}** is the name of the source file to be used in the initial delta. For example, the following command

$ admin -n -iexampl.c s.exampl.c

will use the source file exampl.c as the text to be included in the initial delta of the SCCS file s.exampl.c. The source file specified by **{name}**, exampl.c in the above command line, is not deleted after the text has been included in the SCCS file. It is therefore possible to include the same source file in more than one SCCS file (see Section 10.7).

When **{name}** is not specified, the text for the initial delta is read from standard input until an end-of-file (control D) is reached. This is normally used in connection with pipes, as shown in the following example:

$ cat exampl.c | admin -n -i s.exampl.c

While the above examples have the **-n** option as part of the command line, it is optional. The **-i** option automatically implies the **-n** option. Thus, the following forms of the above examples are also valid commands:

$ admin -iexampl.c s.exampl.c
$ cat exampl.c | admin -i s.exampl.c

Note that a consequence of using the -i option is that only a *single SCCS file* can be created with each execution of the **admin** command.

When the **-i** option is used, the **-r** option can be used to define the SID for the delta. As can be seen in Figure 4.1, SCCS automatically assigns a default value of 1.1 to the SID of the first delta. This may be fine for the first release of a source file, but it may not be relevant when converting the source files for an existing product. For example, if a source file for release 3 of a product is being used for the initial delta, use of the command

$ admin -iexampl.c -r3 s.exampl.c

would create an initial SID of 3.1. This SID would be a more accurate reflection of the current status of the source file than would be the default of 1.1.

Note that the **admin** command will accept any legal value for the SID. It is even possible to assign a value for a branch SID as the name of the initial delta. However, to do this will make creating a trunk delta from the initial delta a very difficult task.

The default comment (see Figure 4.1 for an example) for the initial delta is in the following format:

date and time created /YY/MM/DD HH:MM:SS by login

The **-y{comment}** option allows a different comment to be entered for the initial delta. The following are examples of how to change the initial delta commentary:

$ admin -n -y"initial delta" s.exampl.c
$ admin -iexampl.c -r3 -y"initial delta" s.exampl.c

The **-m** (modification request numbers) option is entered only when the **v{pgm}** flag has been set (see below). The {**mrlist**} is the argument for the **-m** option and is a list of one or more modification request numbers. If the list consists of several numbers, each number is separated from the next by a space or tab. The following examples show how to enter a single number and a list of numbers:

```
$ admin -n -fv -mspr001 s.exampl.c
$ admin -iexampl -fv -m"spr001 spr002" s.exampl.c
```

4.5 Defining the User Table

As mentioned in Chapter 3, the user table lists those users or groups that have permission to make deltas to the SCCS file being created. To establish the user table, the following option of the **admin** command is used:

[-a{login name | numerical group ID}]

Users are defined by their **login name** as specified in the /etc/passwd file. Groups are defined by their **numerical group ID** as specified in the /etc/group file. To show how this option works, we shall use the /etc/passwd file as shown in Figure 4.2 and the /etc/group file shown in Figure 4.3.

As can be seen in Figure 4.1, the default is to have no entries in the user table. Under this condition, anyone who has read permission for the SCCS file

```
      .
      .
      .
bill::101:101:lead programmer team A:/acct/bill:
joe::102:101:librarian team A:/acct/joe:
ted::103:101:jr programmer team A:/acct/ted:
wendy::104:102:lead programmer team B:/acct/wendy:
charlie::105:102:librarian team B:/acct/charlie:
sandy::106:102:programmer team B:/acct/sandy:
      .
      .
      .
```

Figure 4.2   Portion of /etc/passwd File.

```
      .
      .
      .
teamA::101:bill,joe,ted
teamB::102:wendy,charlie,sandy
      .
      .
      .
```

Figure 4.3   Portion of /etc/group File.

and write permission for the directory can make a delta to it. Leaving the detailed discussion of file security until Chapter 10, let's say that the directory mode is 777. With this mode, there is no question that everybody listed in Figure 4.2 has permission to make a delta.

In our first example, team A is the only team to be allowed access to the SCCS file. Since all members of team A belong to the same group, the **numerical group ID** can be used to limit delta permission to team A. The format of the command is

```
$ admin -n -a101 s.exampl.c
```

For our second example, ted is still in training, so only bill and joe are to be given delta permission. The format of the command to accomplish this is

```
$ admin -n -abill -ajoe s.exampl.c
```

Just as someone can be given permission to make a delta, it is possible to specifically deny permission by prefacing the login name or numerical group ID with "**!**". For example, the command

```
$ admin -n -abill -a!joe s.exampl.c
```

or, for **csh** users, the command

```
$ admin -n -abill -a\!joe s.exampl.c
```

grants delta permission to bill and denies delta permission to joe. However, trying to deny delta permission to specific members of a group that have been granted access does not work. The command

```
$ admin -n -a101 -a!ted s.exampl.c
```

still allows ted to have delta permission. Trying to juggle the order of entries in the user table will have no effect; once granted permission, the login has permission.

Warning! The **admin** command does not verify the validity of the data entered. Check your entries with the **prs** command (see Chapter 8) to make sure that IDs have been correctly entered.

4.6 Defining the Flag Table

The flag table is made up of 12 flags. Rather than have each flag set by a separate option, the **-f** option is used to set the various SCCS file flags and has the following format:

[-f{flag}[{flag-val}]]

When we first look at the list of flags that can be defined, we are overwhelmed. What is the purpose of all these flags? When and why should they be set? Part of the confusion is caused by the fact that the flags are usually presented as an alphabetical list. As shown in Table 4.1, the flags fall into five groups. The following sections discuss these flags in more detail. For a descriptive list of the flags, see Appendix A.

TABLE 4.1 CATEGORIES OF SCCS FLAGS

Category	Flag	Definition
Delta access	c	Ceiling release number
	f	Floor release number
	l	Lock release number
Delta creation	b	Branch on leaf delta
	n	Null delta
Get command parameters	d	Default SID
	j	Joint edit
Keyword definitions	i	ID required
	m	Module name
	q	User defined
	t	Module type
Delta command parameters	v	Validate MR number

4.6.1 Delta Access Flags

These flags are used to lock certain deltas from being accessed for the purpose of making another delta. Since it would not make any sense to lock the initial delta, the discussion of these flags will be deferred to Section 7.2.3.

4.6.2 Delta Creation Flags

The delta creation flags group consists of those flags that affect the creation of deltas. When the delta creation flags are not set, SCCS assumes that all deltas are along a single trunk and that delta naming will be as shown in Figure 4.4.

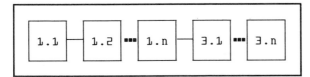

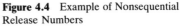

Figure 4.4 Example of Nonsequential Release Numbers

In keeping with the single-trunk approach, the default action for SCCS is not to allow the creation of branch deltas from a leaf delta. If branches from a leaf delta are to be allowed, then the branch flag (**b**) must be set. For a complete discussion on the pros and cons of branching and whether or not the branch flag should be set, see Section 10.6.2.

> There is a great deal of confusion surrounding the meaning of the branch flag. Contrary to the common belief, it does not allow or disallow branching. The setting of this flag only means that it is possible to create a branch delta before a trunk delta is created. For example, if delta 3.2 were a leaf delta, it would be possible to create delta 3.2.1.1 before creating delta 3.3.

As mentioned previously, release numbers are not automatically assigned. Only the **-r** option of the **admin** command, for the initial delta, or the **-r** option of the **get** command (see the next chapter) can be used to change the release number. In fact, SCCS only requires that the Release Numbers be in ascending sequence. For example, deltas could be made with the release numbers of 1 and 3 as shown in Figure 4.4. The null delta flag (**n**) will force null deltas to be created for the missing release numbers. Figure 4.5 shows the resulting delta sequence.

To set these flags, the following command format is used:

$$\$ \text{ admin -n -fb -fn s.exampl.c}$$

As will be seen in Chapter 5, the null deltas created by the null delta flag can be used to create branches based on that release number. Referring to Figure 4.5, it would be possible to create a delta with a SID of 2.1.1.1, although this branch would be equivalent to a branch created from delta 1.n.

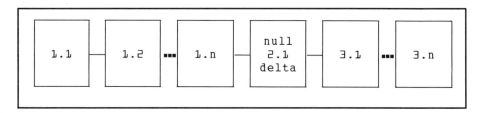

Figure 4.5   Example of Release Numbers with **n** Flag Set.

4.6.3 Get Command Parameter Flags

The name for this group derives from the fact that the flags are used to alter the default parameters for the **get** command. As only the joint edit flag (**j**) relates to the creation of an SCCS file, it will be discussed here. The default SID flag (**d**), which deals with changing the default SID on an active file, will be discussed in Chapter 7 on SCCS file maintenance.

One main feature of SCCS is that the **-e** option of the **get** command, by default, allows only one copy of a particular SID to be open for edit at any one time. This feature is how SCCS protects the integrity of the relationship between different generations of a file. For example, if programmer A has retrieved version 3.2 and the delta to be created is 3.3, then no one else can retrieve 3.2 for editing. While this is correct when branching is not allowed, it may present too great a limitation when branching is allowed for leaf deltas.

The joint edit (**j**) flag overrides this requirement so that more than the one copy of the same SID can be retrieved for editing. Then the only requirement is that no two copies result in the creation of a delta with the same SID. This restriction means that the same parent SID can have different children being edited at the same time as long as they are on different branches. To set the flag while creating an SCCS file, the following command is used:

$ admin -n -fb -fj s.exampl.c

Note that the joint edit flag does not require that the branch flag be set. Once a **get -e** has been made to create a direct descendant, the **j** flag will allow branches to be created from the leaf delta whether or not the branch flag has been set. The assumption is that the delta for the direct descendant will be made at some time in the future.

4.6.4 Keyword Definition Flags

IDentification keywords are variables placed into a source file, which are then replaced by the specified information when the file is retrieved. This group of flags relates to the requirement for the presence of ID keywords and the content of certain ID keywords.

As part of the processing of a source file, the **get** and **delta** commands check to see if the source file contains an SCCS identification keyword string (for details, see Chapter 8 on How to Use SCCS Information). If the string is not present, the message "No id keywords (ge6)" will be issued. The default is to treat this as a warning message. However, the lack of an identification keyword string can be changed to a fatal error by setting the ID required flag (**i**).

Starting with UNIX System V, the capability of the **i** flag has been expanded to include an ID keyword verification string. The format for the **i** flag is

-fi[{ID keyword string}]

where the variable {**ID keyword string**} represents the string that must exist in the source file.

For example, the command

$ **admin -n -fi s.exampl.c**

merely requires that an ID keyword string exist in the source file whenever a **get** or **delta** command is executed. However, by expanding the command to

$ **admin -n -fi"%Z% %M% %I% %D%" s.exampl.c**

the test now verifies that the ID keyword string has the correct format.

Note, the actual test is only for the length of the {**ID keyword string**}. Thus, if the source file contained the string "%Z% %M% %I% %D% %T%", it would be considered a valid string. So, while the {ID keyword string} can be used to test for compliance to standards, it should be considered a minimal compliance test and not an exact compliance test. See Section 10.7 for a more complete discussion of ID keyword standards.

The **m**, **q**, and **t** flags provide additional information that can be used in ID keyword strings and for use by the **prs** command (see Chapter 8). These flags perform no control function, and their value and use are determined by the SCCS administrator. The module name (**m**) flag changes the *module name* variable, which has a default value of the SCCS file name with the prefix of "**s.**" removed. The module type (**t**) flag assigns a value to the *type of module* variable. The user defined (**q**) flag is an undefined variable whose use and contents are at the discretion of the SCCS administrator. Suggestions on how to use these variables will be discussed in Chapter 10 on Building the SCCS Source Tree. These three flags have the following formats:

-**fm**{module name}
-**ft**{type of module}
-**fq**{user defined text}

The following examples show how to set these variables:

$ **admin -n -fmnewprg s.exampl.c**
$ **admin -n -ftc s.exampl.c**
$ **admin -n -fq"string example" s.exampl.c**

4.6.5 Delta Command Parameter Flags

Just as the get command parameter flags altered the default action of the **get** command, the delta command parameter flags alter the default action of the **delta** command. This group consists of only one flag, the validate MR (**v**) flag, but that one flag plays a major role in the degree to which SCCS is integrated into a total project control system. The format for the **v** flag is as follows:

-fv[{validation pgm}]

The default is for the delta command not to require the entry of modification request numbers when adding a delta. If this flag is set, then modification request (MR) numbers must be entered by either the **-m** option of the **delta** command or when the **delta** command prompts for the numbers. If the optional {**validation pgm**} name is entered, the **delta** command will pass the MR numbers to the program or shell script for validation (see Appendix D for an example of an MR validation program). If the exit status of the {**validation pgm**} is not equal to zero, **delta** will abort with a fatal error. The following are examples of how the flag could be used:

```
$ admin -n -fv -mMR001 s.exampl.c
$ admin -n -fvmrval -mMR002 s.exampl.c
```

As can be seen, SCCS provides for three levels of problem tracking:

1. No tracking: the default.
2. Informational tracking: the **v** flag with no validation program.
3. Full integration of source control and MR tracking system: the **v** flag linked to an MR validation program. If you choose to do so, the simple example program shown in Appendix D could be expanded to integrate into a full tracking system.

4.7 Loading the Descriptive Text

The format of this option is

-t{text file}

When creating an SCCS file, the variable {**text file**} is required: it is the name of the file whose contents are to be inserted into the descriptive text section of the SCCS file. To illustrate this concept, we use a file called **note.txt** whose contents are as shown in Figure 4.6. The command

$ admin -n -tnote.txt s.exampl.c

will insert the contents of **note.txt** into the descriptive text section of the SCCS file **s.exampl.c** as shown in Figure 4.7.

```
Standard text segment to be included in all SCCS files.
The text relates to the SCCS file and can only be displayed
by using the :FD: variable of the prs command.
```

Figure 4.6   Sample Text in File note.txt

```
@h21982
@s 00000/00000/00000
@d D 1.1 89/02/03 09:27:26 pgmr1 1 0
@c date and time created 89/02/03 09:27:26 by pgmr1
@e
@u
@U
@t
Standard text segment to be included in all SCCS files.
The text relates to the SCCS file and can only be displayed
by using the :FD: variable of the prs command.
@T
@I 1
@E 1
```

Figure 4.7 SCCS File with Descriptive Text Section

4.8 Helpful Hints

1. One problem with all SCCS files being self-contained is that updates for common entries can be a tedious task. One of these entries is the login names for the user table. Entry of login names can be made much simpler by using the numerical group ID in place of the login names. This way only the /etc/group file has to be maintained instead of every SCCS file. However, this only works when the groups with read permission and write permission are identical (see Section 10.4).

2. Another problem with the self-contained file concept is that the command line to create an SCCS file can become rather cumbersome. For example, to define an initial delta and all the parameters, the following command line might be required:

```
$ admin -iexmpl.c -r4 -y"initial comment" -mMR01 \
> -a101 -fb -fi"%Z%%M% %I% %Y% %D%" -fvmrchck \
> -tnote.txt s.exmpl.c
```

If the above had to be typed for every file, initializing SCCS would be a monstrous task. To reduce typing, you can use **csh** to establish an alias with the file names as arguments. Or a shell script can be written that defines the standard parameters and has the others as variables (see Chapter 10 for an example).

3. Using the {**ID keyword string**} variable of the **i** flag has its consequences. See Chapter 7 for information on what happens when the value of the variable is changed after the file has been created.

CHAPTER 5

Retrieving
a Source File
The "get" Command

5.1 Introduction

To be usable by any other UNIX utility such as the C compiler or troff, a source file must be retrieved from its SCCS file via the **get** command. Furthermore, the **get** command is the only command that can retrieve a source file from an SCCS file and must be executed prior to the use of the **delta** command. Since its only function is to retrieve a source file from an SCCS file, the **get** command does not alter the SCCS file.

To be as flexible as possible, the **get** command has options to control:

- Which delta is retrieved
- What delta will be created
- The mode of the output and its format

5.2 Command Syntax

The format for the **get** command is as follows:

get [-r{SID}] [-i{include list}] [-x{exclude list}][-t]
[-a{seq-no}] [-c{cutoff}] [-g] [-l[p]] [-p] [-s]
[-k] [-m] [-n] [-w{string}] [-e] [-b] {file . . .}

The following sections are organized to discuss the options by groups, starting with a simple **get** with no options. Each group will show how the default action of the **get** command can be modified to produce different results. Since the **-e** (retrieve for edit) option depends on what is retrieved for edit, all the options dealing with source file retrieval will be dealt with before the options that affect editing.

Throughout the remainder of the book, the following naming conventions will be used for the components of the SID:

- The *release number* will be represented by an **R**.
- The *level number* will be represented by an **L**.
- The *branch number* will be represented by a **B**.
- The *sequence number* will be represented by an **S**.
- If any of the above is prefixed by an **m**, it means that the *maximum number* defined in the SCCS file will be used.

Using Figure 5.1 as an example, **mR.mL** would refer to the SID 3.2. Or, if we are talking about the branch, then **R.L.B.mS** would refer to the SID 1.3.1.3. To avoid any unnecessary confusion, this is the same as the naming convention used in the AT&T SCCS documentation.

5.3 No Options: The Default Parameters

The simplest form of the command is

get {file . . .}

where the argument {**file . . .**} follows the rules for file names discussed in Section 2.4.

If the default SID has not been modified by the **admin** (see the discussion of the **d** flag in Section 7.2.3) command, the SID retrieved will be equal to the SID defined by **mR.mL** (the Maximum Release and the Maximum Level within that release). If a different default SID has been defined by the **d** flag, then the SID retrieved will follow the rules defined by the **-r** option as described in Section 5.4.1.

The retrieved source file is written to the **g-file** (get file), which is the name of the SCCS file with the "**s.**" prefix removed. The **g-file** is created in the current working directory and will have a file mode of **444** (no write permission). The owner of the file will be the real user (see the Glossary for the difference between real and effective users).

The following summary information about the retrieved source file is directed to the standard output:

[<**SCCS File Name**>] (Printed when multiple files are involved)
<**SID Retrieved**>
<**Number of Lines**> lines

After printing the preceding, any [**<error messages>**] are directed to standard error.

    To show how the different options of SCCS are related, the delta tree shown in Figure 5.1 will be the basis for all the examples in this chapter. To see how it works, we can start by executing the command

$ get s.exampl.c

The **get** command will create a **g-file** called exampl.c, and it will be the retrieved source file for SID 3.2 (**mR.mL**). Since only a single file was retrieved, the following will be printed on the standard output and standard error:

3.2
23 lines
No id keywords (ge6)

Note that the last message would be printed only if the **get** command did not find any **ID**entification keywords (see Chapter 8).

    If the following **get** command was executed,

$ get s.exampl.c s.test.c

where both files contained **ID**entification keywords, then the following would be printed on the standard output:

s.exampl.c:
3.2
23 lines

s.text.c:
3.1
45 lines

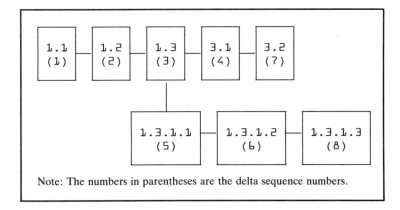

Note: The numbers in parentheses are the delta sequence numbers.

Figure 5.1.   SID Chart for SCCS File s.exampl.c

Using a simple **get** command as the basis, we can start modifying it by adding various options to provide different results.

5.4 Controlling the Delta to Be Retrieved

To retrieve any other SID than that specified by **mR.mL**, we need to specify what delta to retrieve. The **get** command provides four different options for determining the SID to be retrieved:

-r   Specify the delta name
-t   Retrieve the top SID
-a   Specify the delta sequence number
-c   Retrieve according to a cutoff date

In addition, other deltas can be included into the retrieved source file with the **-i** option. And/or deltas may be excluded from the retrieved source file with the **-x** option. The following sections will discuss each of these options.

5.4.1 Specifying the SID

The **-r** option is by far the most common way of specifying an alternate SID. The format for this option is

-r{SID}

where the {**SID**} can be any one of the following forms: **R**, **R.L**, **R.L.B**, or **R.L.B.S**. What SID is retrieved with each of the forms is explained below.

    The variables **R.L** or **R.L.B.S** identify a specific SID that must exist. If the SID does not exist, then the **get** command will fail. Referring to Figure 5.1,

```
$ get -r1.2 s.exampl.c
$ get -r3.2 s.exampl.c
$ get -r1.3.1.2 s.exampl.c
```

are valid statements, and the **g-file** will contain the source file for specified SID, whereas

```
$ get -r2.2 s.exampl.c
$ get -r1.3.1.6 s.exampl.c
```

are not valid statements.

    The variables **R** or **R.L.B** are a bit more complicated in that the last component of the SID is unknown and must be resolved by the **get** command. For the variable **R.L.B**, the rule is that **R.L.B** must reference an existing branch. If the branch exists, then the SID represented by **R.L.B.mS** will be retrieved. Thus, the command

$ get -r1.3.1 s.exampl.c

retrieves the SID 1.3.1.3. When only **R** is given, one of three things can happen:

1. If **R** exists, then the SID represented by **R.mL** is retrieved. For example, the command

   $ get -r1 s.exampl.c

   would retrieve the SID 1.3.
2. If **R** does not exist and **R** is less than **mR**, then the highest **R** less than **R** is used. This is called the **hR**. The version retrieved is then referred to as **hR.mL**. For example, since the release number 2 has not been defined in Figure 5.1, the command

   $ get -r2 s.exampl.c

   will retrieve the SID 1.3.
3. If **R** does not exist and **R** is greater than **mR**, then the SID represented by **mR.mL** is retrieved. Although the SID retrieved is the same as if the **-r** option had not been given, when combined with the **-e** option this will result in the changing of the release number for the next delta.

The above actions are summarized in Table 5.1. Included in this table are a few notes as to the purpose for using the different variations of the SID.

5.4.2 Specifying the Top SID

If the command

$ get -t s.exampl.c

is entered, the source file retrieved will be **mR.mL**. This is no different than what would be retrieved if the flag was not present. However, when used in combination with the **-r** option, it will retrieve the latest delta based on the pattern given. The following are the rules used by the **-t** option:

1. If no **-r** option is given, then the SID retrieved will be **mR.mL**. However, if the **d** flag has been set for the SCCS file, the default SID is treated the same as if it were the argument to the **-r** option.
2. If **R** is the only argument given to the **-r** option, then the SID retrieved will be either **R.mL** or **R.L.B.mS**, depending on what was the last delta made for the specified release. For instance, the command

$ get -t -r1 s.exampl.c

TABLE 5.1 SID RETRIEVAL TABLE

{SID}	Rules for retrieval	SID retrieved	Notes
R	Exist: yes	R.mL	Can be used to retrieve source files for a specific release. It can also be used with the **-e** option to start a branch from the **mL** of an **R** < **mR**.
R	Exist: no and R < mR	hR.mL	In conjunction with the above, a good way to get the latest release of a source file when retrieving an entire directory.
R	Exist: no	mR.mL	The primary purpose of this form is to change the release number for the next delta.
R.L	Exist: yes	R.L	Required to retrieve exact SID wanted when building a product. It also comes in handy when a branch is to be created from a SID that is less than the SID defined by mR.mL.
R.L.B	Exist: yes	R.L.B.mS	The simplest way to retrieve the last SID from a branch.
R.L.B.S	Exist: yes	R.L.B.S	The reasons for using this form are the same as those for R.L.

would retrieve the SID 1.3.1.3 because it is the latest delta made with the release number of 1.

3. If the argument to the **-r** option is given as **R.L**, then the delta retrieved will be the last delta with that pattern. Unless one or more branches are connected to the delta specified by **R.L**, the delta retrieved would be the delta defined by **R.L**. For example, the command

        $ get -t -r1.2 s.exampl.c

will retrieve delta 1.2. However, if there are branches, the delta retrieved will be **R.L.B.mS**. This is obvious, since a branch delta by definition has to be of more recent vintage than the trunk delta. The only question is what is the latest branch delta. From Figure 5.1, the command

        $ get -t -r1.3 s.exampl.c

will retrieve the delta 1.3.1.3.

4. Using the argument **R.L.B** for the **-r** option produces the same result as if the **-t** option were not present. With this pattern the only delta that can be retrieved is **R.L.B.mS**.

5. While it will not fail, specifying an argument of **R.L.B.S** is a waste of time, as there is only one possible pattern that can be matched.

Is this option of any real value? If there are no branches, then the result will always be the same as if only the **-r** option is used. So the only possible value is when there are branches in the SCCS file. The one useful function of the **-t** option is that it is the quickest way to see if a trunk delta is the connecting point for any branches. However, if it is information about the SCCS file that is needed, use the **prs** command (see Chapter 8).

> **Warning!** Never use this option in combination with the **-e**; it is a bit like playing Russian roulette. At the outset, you have no, or at least very little, knowledge of the end result.

5.4.3 Specifying the Delta Sequence Number

The format of this option is

-a{seq-no}

where {**seq-no**} is the delta sequence number of the delta. As previously stated, in addition to the SID, which is used for external reference, each delta in an SCCS file has a delta sequence number that is used by the SCCS commands.

This option is used in the **get** commands generated by the **comb** command (see Chapter 7) and, if used for any other purpose, must be used with great care. It is particularly dangerous when combined with the **-e** option (see below), since the naming of SID for the delta follows the conventions used by the **-r** option. If you don't know the SID, then why edit this delta? The end result could be another leaf delta along the trunk or branch, or it could result in a new branch. After all, the delta sequence number does not convey any information about the delta. My best advice is don't use the option.

5.4.4 Specifying the Cutoff Date

The format of this option is

-c{cutoff}

where {**cutoff**} specifies the cutoff date and time. The format of {**cutoff**} is as follows:

YY[MM[DD[HH[MM[SS]]]]]

While the cutoff date and time could be specified as **-c881009140200**, they could also be specified as "**-c88/10/9 14:02:00**". The rule is that, as long as the option is enclosed in double quotation marks, each element of the cutoff date and time can be separated from the next by any nonnumeric character.

Not all elements of the date and time need be specified. However, if an element is not specified, it defaults to its maximum value. Table 5.2 shows the variations of the different elements and the resulting default.

If the command

$ get -c881130 s.exampl.c

is executed, then the SID retrieved will be the **hR.hL** (highest release number and highest level number within the release) that was less than or equal to the cutoff date and time specified. If we were trying to find a branch delta less than the cutoff date, then the command would have to be combined with the **-r** option, using the form **R.L.B** to specify the branch. For example, the command

$ get -r1.3.1 -c881130 s.exampl.c

will find the SID meeting the requirement of **R.L.B.hS**, where **hS** is the highest sequence number that has a date that is less than or equal to the cutoff date.

Note that, since we do not know which SID will be retrieved, this command should never be used in combination with the **-e** option.

TABLE 5.2 CUTOFF DATE AND TIME EXAMPLES

{cutoff}	Example	Defaults to:
YY	88	88/12/31 23:59:59
YYMM	88/11	88/11/30 23:59:59
YYMMDD	88/11/15	88/11/15 23:59:59
YYMMDDHH	88/11/15 14	88/11/15 14:59:59
YYMMDDHHMM	88/11/15 14:30	88/11/15 14:30:59

5.4.5 Including Other SIDs

The format for this option is

-i{include list}

where {**include list**} has the following syntax:

```
{include list} = R.L | R.L.B.S | {range} [, . . .]
{range} = R.L1 − R.L2 or
R.L − R or
R.L.B.S1 − R.L.B.S2 or
R.L.B.S − R.L.B
```

The above syntax statement looks rather imposing, but it is really straightforward. When an individual SID is specified, it must reference a specific SID (**R.L** or **R.L.B.S**) and not an ambiguous SID (**R** or **R.L.B**). If a range is specified, the starting point must be a specific SID, and the end can either be a specific SID or an ambiguous SID. If you compare the above to the UNIX documentation, you will see that the syntax for the {**include list**} is different. The UNIX documentation implies that the individual SID or the starting SID of a range can be an ambiguous SID, but such is not the case.

This option only has meaning when branches exist in the SCCS file. As discussed in Chapter 3, starting from any existing SID, the source file is the sum of all deltas on its path back to the null file. Using Figure 5.1, if SID 3.2 were to be retrieved, then the deltas identified by SID 1.1, 1.2, 1.3, 3.1, and 3.2 would automatically be included. Without branches, there would be no other delta to include. However, with branching, it is possible that the change made to create delta 1.3.1.3 needs to be included when making the next delta on the trunk. The reverse also applies where a trunk delta is to be included in a branch. The following are a few examples of how the **-i** option might be used.

To include a branch delta into the trunk, the command is

$ get -i1.3.1.3 s.exampl.c

Conversely, the following command will include a delta from the trunk into a branch:

$ get -r1.3.1 -i3.1 s.exampl.c

To include a range of deltas from the trunk into a branch, the command is

$ get -r1.3.1 -i3.1-3 s.exampl.c

or

$ get -r1.3.1 -i3.1,3.2 s.exampl.c

either of which would include the deltas named 3.1 and 3.2 into the source file made up from delta 1.3.1.3. Specifying a range of branch deltas takes the form

$ get -i1.3.1.2-1.3.1 s.exampl.c

which would include the deltas named 1.3.1.2 and 1.3.1.3 into the deltas that make up the source file from delta 3.2.

The information printed on standard output is modified to indicate the deltas that have been included in building the new source file. For example, the last **get** command produces the following output:

```
= = = = = = = = = = = = = = = =
Included:
1.3.1.2
1.3.1.3
= = = = = = = = = = = = = = = =
3.2
45 lines
```

Including deltas from one path into another can generate conflicts. The most common form of conflict occurs when a delta in the normal path modifies the same lines in the source file as did one of the deltas that was included. If this occurs, SCCS prints an "Inex" (Include Exclude) conflict message on standard error that indicates the beginning line number and ending line number of the conflict. The following is an example of the error output when a conflict occurs:

```
$ get -i1.3.1.3 s.exampl.c
= = = = = = = = = = = = = = = =
Included:
1.3.1.3
= = = = = = = = = = = = = = = =
3.2
Inex conflict begins at line 6 (co25)
Inex conflict ends at line 9 (co26)
63 lines
```

In most cases, the conflicts can be easily resolved since the source file contains the lines from all the deltas that were in conflict. If identifying the correct lines is too difficult, the **-m** option (see below) can be used to identify which lines belong to which SID.

The **-i** option can be a boon to the management of changes to trunks and branches. However, it does carry a price tag. With the ability to make a change in one path and have it included in another path goes the requirement that deltas be sets of changes that are applicable to all paths. If a delta consists of any changes that are specific to that branch, then the use of the **-i** option is not advisable. Using Figure 5.1 as an example, if SID 1.3.1.3 fixes a problem that also needs to be fixed in the trunk, then it can be included with SID 3.2 to create SID 3.3. However, if the deltas to be included contain any other unrelated changes, these changes have to be removed after the delta has been included. Depending on the extent of the changes that are not relevant to the trunk, this can be either a simple or complicated task.

5.4.6 Excluding Default SIDs

The opposite of including deltas is the exclude option, which has the format

-x{exclude list}

where **{exclude list}** has the same syntax as the **{include list}** described above.

When a delta is to be excluded, it must be a delta that is part of the ancestry of the delta being retrieved. For example, if SID 3.2 was being retrieved, then 1.2 might be excluded. But it would serve no purpose to exclude 1.3.1.1, since it was not included in the first place. Yet the **get** command will not issue any error messages for any extraneous exclude options. It should be noted that excluding a file on one path has no effect on any other path. For example, the commands

```
$ get -e -x1.2 s.exampl.c
$ delta s.exampl.c
```

create a delta named 3.3 that will automatically exclude delta 1.2 if it is retrieved. Yet this change has no impact on the future progeny of the branch 1.3.1.

As can be seen from the above, the primary use of this option is to permanently delete a delta that is one of the ancestors of the delta being retrieved. If the most current delta has to be deleted, for example 3.2, then the **rmdel** command is used instead of creating a new delta 3.3 that excludes 3.2.

As with the include option, any conflicts that arise as a result of excluding a delta will be written to standard error in the same format as the include option. If multiple changes have been made to one section of a source file, then excluding an old ancestor can create conflicts that are difficult to resolve. Again, the **-m** option can be used to help resolve any conflicts.

5.5 Controlling the Mode of Output

The default action for the **get** command is to place the retrieved source into the **g-file** and send all messages to standard output. The **-g**, **-l**, **-p**, and **-s** options can be used to alter these output modes as follows:

- The **-g** option suppresses creation of the **g-file**.
- The **-p** option directs the **g-file** to standard output.
- The **-s** option suppresses informational messages.
- The **-l** option creates a delta summary file.

The following is a more detailed discussion of each of these options.

The **-g** option suppresses the actual retrieval of the source file from the SCCS file. As a result, the **g-file** is not created. This command is useful for several reasons:

1. The most common use is when a **p-file** needs to be created because it was accidentally removed or because a new version of a source file has been received and it needs to be stored in the SCCS file (remember, a **get** must precede a **delta**).
2. Only the **l-file** (see below) is needed.
3. It can also be used to verify the existence of a particular SID. Using the **get** command for this purpose was necessary with UNIX Version 7. However, with UNIX System V, the **val** command is better suited to this task.

The **-p** option redirects the retrieved source file to standard output instead of creating a **g-file**. The output that would have been sent to the standard output is redirected to standard error. If redirection did not occur, the messages from the **get** command would be interleaved with the retrieved text. This option serves a number of useful functions:

1. If the filename of the source file is to be different than the default name given to the **g-file**, then the output can be redirected to a named file. This would be necessary in cases needing more than one version of a source file at one time, or when one source file is to be modified to create a different source file. In the latter case, the ID keywords must not be expanded (see Chapter 8). This is done by combining the **-p** option with the **-k** option (see below). For example, the command

    $ get -k -p s.exampl.c > test.c

    would retrieve the SID identified by **mR.mL** and create the file test.c.

2. In some situations, it may be necessary to direct the output through a pipe to another command. For example, the command

    $ get -p s.exampl.c | grep expression

    would search the source file for **expression**.

The **-s** option suppresses all output that goes to the standard output. If the **-p** option is also present, it will also suppress the output directed to standard error, except for fatal error messages. Looking back at the last example, the output of the **grep** command would be mixed with the messages from the **get** command. To prevent this from happening, the command should be

    $ get -p -s s.exampl.c | grep expression

The final option in this group is the **-l** option, which actually has the format of **-l[p]**. The **-l** option causes a delta summary report in the format shown in Table 5.3 to be written to the **l-file**. The **l-file** will have the leading **s** of the SCCS file name replaced with an **l**. The file will be created in the current working directory and will have a file mode of 444, and the owner will be the real user. For example, the command

    $ get -g -l s.exampl.c

will create a delta summary file called **l.exampl.c**, the contents of which would look something like Figure 5.2.

Note that the **-g** option will cause only the **l-file** to be created. Changing the option to **-lp** will cause the same report to be sent to standard output, and no **l-file** will be created. With this option the standard output needs to be suppressed,

TABLE 5.3 I-FILE FORMAT

Line no.	Field no.	Description
1	1	Field will be blank if delta was applied or an * if it was not.
1	2	Field will be blank if the delta was applied or was ignored. If the delta was not applied, but for reasons other than being ignored, then it will contain an *.
1	3	Will contain a letter indicating the reason why a delta was or was not applied. The letters and their meanings are: I, included E, excluded C, cutoff
1	4	One space character.
1	5	SID of the delta.
1	6	Tab character.
1	7	Date and time the delta was created in the format YY/MM/DD HH:MM:SS.
1	8	One space character.
1	9	Login name of the person who made the delta as defined in the delta table.
2	1	Tab character.
2	2	Delta comment.
3	1	Tab character.
3	2	MR numbers.

Note: 1. If more than one comment has been entered for the delta, the line 2 format will be repeated for each comment line.

   2. If more than one MR record exists for the delta, then the line 2 format will be repeated for each MR record present for the delta.

```
 **   1.3.1.3      89/02/06  18:04:32 pgmr1
          example 8
          mr008
      3.2 89/02/06  18:03:14 pgmr1
          example 7
          mr007
 **   1.3.1.2      89/02/06  18:02:03 pgmr1
          example 6
          mr006
   .
   .
   .

      1.1 89/02/06  08:13:00 pgmr1
          example 1
          mr001
```

Figure 5.2 Example of **-l** Output

so the **-s** option should be combined with the **-lp** option, as shown in the following example, to suppress the normal **get** command output.

$ get -g -lp -s s.exampl.c

5.6 Controlling the Output Format

This section discusses those flags that affect the format of the **g-file**. Normally, the **get** command will alter the stored format of the SCCS file by expanding the ID keywords. The flags that alter this format are as follows:

> **-k**   Suppress expansion of ID keywords
> **-w**   Alter the %W% ID keyword
> **-m**   Prefix each line with SID
> **-n**   Prefix each line with module name

Of the options discussed in this section, the most useful is the **-k** option, which is used to suppress the replacement of ID keywords during source file retrieval. Although the subject of ID keywords will be covered in detail in Chapter 8, ID keywords are the names of variables that are replaced with the appropriate SCCS information when the file is retrieved. For example, if exampl.c contained the ID keyword string "%Z%%M% %I%", the **get** command would normally substitute the string with the equivalent data to create the string "@(#)exampl.c 3.2". However, if the **-k** option is specified, the ID keyword substitution is suppressed, just as substitution is suppressed with the **-e** option. Also, the **g-file** is created with a file mode of 644, which gives write permission to the real owner. Thus, except for the creation of a **p-file**, it is the same as using the **-e** option.

This option is useful in the following circumstances:

1. In conjunction with the **-p** option (as described above), it can be used to create a new source file with a different file name.
2. Let's say that a source file has already been retrieved for editing. For any number of reasons, the file is lost or, in order to start with a clean slate, the source file needs to be retrieved again. Instead of deleting the **p-file** and starting all over again, it is much easier and safer to get another copy using the **-k** option in place of the **-e** option.

The **-w** option can be used to alter the %W% ID keyword, which is a shorthand notation for the ID keyword string described above. The format of the option is as follows:

-w{string}

The string substitution occurs before the ID keyword string is expanded. Thus, if the {**string**} did not contain any ID keywords, get would issue the "No id keywords" message. However, the {**string**} could contain a different ID keyword string, which would then be expanded.

Note that the **-w** option has no effect if the **-k** or **-e** options are also present on the command line.

The **-m** option is used to prefix each line of retrieved text with the SID of the delta that last changed the line. Thus, the format for each line is as follows:

<SID><horizontal tab>text line

While rarely used, this option can come in handy when trying to resolve a conflict arising out of the use of the **-i** or **-x** options.

If the command

$ get -p -s s\.* | grep program

is given, the output might look like the following:

```
The program can be used for . . . .
Which program should be used . . . .
The program needs to be identified . . .
```

Given this output, it would not be possible to identify which source files produced the lines that matched the string. Adding the **-n** option to the **get** command will prefix each line with the module name, followed by a horizontal tab. By using the command

$ get -p -s -n s\.* | grep program

the output produced would look like the following:

```
exmpl–1.t    The program can be used for . . . .
exmpl–3.t    Which program should be used . . . .
exmpl–8.t    The program needs to be identified . . .
```

However, if the **m** flag has been set, then the <module name> will be the value for the flag (see Chapter 4). Also, if the **-m** and **-n** options are both given, the format of the retrieved line is

<module name><horizontal tab><SID><horizontal tab>text line

Obviously, if you don't want this information to become a permanent part of the source file, the **-m** and **-n** options must never be used with the **-e** option.

5.7 Editing a Source File

The **-e** option is a declaration of an intent to make a delta. As such, the use of this option imposes the following additional restrictions:

1. The user table of the SCCS file is checked to verify that the login name of the user executing the **get** is in the list. If the user table is empty, then all users who have write permission in the SCCS file directory will have permission to make a delta.
2. The release number (**R**) is checked to see that it is greater than or equal to the floor and less than or equal to the ceiling release numbers as defined in the SCCS file (see the **f** and **c** flags in Chapter 4).
3. The release number (**R**) cannot be locked (see the **l** flag of the **admin** command in Chapter 4).

If the above tests are passed, then the following five functions are performed:

1. It suppresses the expansion of the ID keywords (see the description of the **-k** option above).
2. If the **p-file** does not exist for the SCCS file, then one is created in the same directory as the SCCS file with a file mode of 644, and the owner is the effective user.
3. If the **p-file** exists, it checks to see that the same SID has not already been retrieved for edit. This requirement can be turned off with the joint edit (**j**) flag (see Chapter 4). If the joint edit flag is set, then the same SID can be retrieved for edit as long as it does not create a duplicate delta SID.
4. A record is added to the **p-file**, which will be used by the **delta** command in building an entry in the delta table of the SCCS file.
5. If neither the **-g** or **-p** option is present, the **g-file** will be created with a file mode of 644. Thus, the real user, who is the owner of the file, will have write permission. If a writable **g-file** is already present in the current working directory, the **get** will fail, unless either the **-g** or **-p** option is also part of the command line.

The **p-file** is the key to the **-e** option because it provides the **delta** command with the necessary information to make a delta, as shown in Table 5.4. Of the

TABLE 5.4 FORMAT OF p-FILE

Field no.	Description
1	SID of retrieved delta
2	One space character
3	SID of new delta (delta SID)
4	One space character
5	Login name of the real user
6	One space character
7	Date and time that the **get** command was executed in the format YY/MM/DD HH:MM:SS
8	One space character
9	The argument for the **-i** option, if present
10	One space character
11	The argument for the **-x** option, if present

elements in the file, the only one that needs more explanation is the SID of the delta to be made. The following should make this seemingly confusing subject a little clearer.

The delta SID depends on the SID retrieved and whether or not the **-b** option is present. If the **-b** option is not present, then the rules for naming the delta SID are as follows:

1. Barring other conditions, the delta SID will continue along the same path as the retrieved SID. Thus, if the **mR.mL** is the SID retrieved, then the delta SID will be **mR.(mL + 1)**. Similarly, for branches, if **R.L.B.mS** is retrieved, then the delta SID will be **R.L.B.(mS + 1)**. Referring back to Figure 5.1, **mR.mL** is equal to 3.2, so the delta SID is 3.3. The SID 1.3.1.3 is the SID specified by **R.L.B.mS**, so the delta SID will be named 1.3.1.4.

2. If the argument of the **-r** option is **R** and R > mR, then the delta SID will be named **R.1**, since it will be the first delta in a new release.

3. If the SID retrieved is not **mR.mL**, then a branch must be created based on the delta retrieved. If this did not happen, then the delta SID created based on incrementing the level number will either create a duplicate SID or force the SID to not match chronological events. For example, if the retrieved SID was 1.2, the delta SID could not be 1.3, as that would create a duplicate SID. However, if the retrieved SID was 1.3, then to name the new SID 1.4 will give the allusion that 3.1 included 1.4 as part of its heritage. Thus, a branch is created, with the name of the delta SID being **R.L.(mB + 1).1**, where the **R.L** is the same as that of the retrieved SID.

4. To prevent duplicate SIDs in branches, if the SID retrieved is not **R.L.B.mS**, then delta SID must be created as a separate branch. The name of the delta SID will follow the same rules as in rule 3 above.

While the **-b** option can be given at any time, it only has meaning when the retrieved delta is a leaf delta and the branch flag has been set in the flag table. If the **-b** option is present and the conditions mentioned above have been met, then a new branch will be created that has the same **R.L** as the retrieved delta. Regardless of whether the retrieved delta is from the trunk or a branch, the delta SID will be named **R.L.(mB + 1).1**. For example, if the retrieved SID is 3.2, which is a leaf delta, then the delta SID would be 3.2.1.1. Following the same rule, if the retrieved SID is 1.3.1.3, the delta SID would be 1.3.2.1.

If the branch flag has not been set in the flag table, then the **-b** option is ignored and the delta SID is named according to the rules mentioned previously.

Note: The **get** command does not issue an error or warning message when the **-b** option has been ignored.

But what is to prevent two SCCS commands from updating the same SCCS file or the same **p-file** at the same time? The method used by SCCS is that the **admin** (see Chapters 4 and 7), **get**, **delta** (see Chapter 6), **cdc** (see Chapter 7), and **rmdel** (see Chapter 7) commands create a **z-file** while they are updating the SCCS file or the **p-file**. If a **z-file** is present, then the command will wait until the **z-file** is deleted. The **z-file** contains the process number of the command being executed and is deleted when the command is finished executing. The name of the **z-file** is the same as that of the SCCS file, with the prefix changed from "**s.**" to "**z.**", and is created in the same directory as that which contains the SCCS file.

The final step for a **get -e** is to print the following summary information about the retrieved source on the standard output:

```
[<SCCS File Name>] (Printed when for multiple files)
[= = = = = = = = = = = = = = =
Included:
<argument of -i>
= = = = = = = = = = = = = = = = =]
[= = = = = = = = = = = = = = =
Excluded:
<argument of -x>
= = = = = = = = = = = = = = = = =]
<SID Retrieved>
new delta <SID of New Delta>
<Number of Lines> lines
[<error messages>]
```

For example, the command

```
$ get -e -r1.3.1 -i3.1 -x1.2 s.exampl.c
```

will print the following information:

```
= = = = = = = = = = = = = = = =
Included:
3.1
= = = = = = = = = = = = = = = =
= = = = = = = = = = = = = = = =
Excluded:
1.2
= = = = = = = = = = = = = = = =
1.3.1.3
new delta 1.3.1.4
342 Lines
```

5.8 Canceling a "get -e"

Once a **get -e** has been made, the **p-file** will continue to exist until a delta is made, the **p-file** has been manually deleted (a bad practice), or an **unget** command has been executed. The **unget** command is the best way of canceling an intent to make a delta. It takes care of the **p-file** and deletes the **g-file**. The format for this command is as follows:

unget [-n] [-r{SID}] [-s] {file . . .}

The argument {**file . . .**} follows the rules for SCCS file names defined in Section 2.4.

When **unget** is executed, it automatically deletes the **g-file**. If the **g-file** is to be kept, then the command has to be executed with the **-n** option.

In most cases, the **p-file** consists of only the record for the delta to be deleted. However, if branches have been created, it is possible for more than one record to exist in the **p-file**. When this happens, the **unget** command needs to know which record to delete. This is accomplish by using the **-r{SID}** option, where {**SID**} is the delta SID. For reasons to be explained in the next chapter, the delta SID uniquely identifies the record to be deleted.

When **unget** completes the deletion of the **p-file**, it prints the delta SID on the standard output. To suppress this message, include the **-s** option on the command line.

5.9 Helpful Hints

1. A word of caution: not all of the options previously discussed make sense when used with the **-e** option. These are the **-a**, **-c**, **-k**, **-m**, **-n**, **-p**, and **-t** options.

2. Although it is easy to just remove the **p-file** as a way of canceling an edit, remember that one **p-file** is created for each SCCS file even though more than one new delta may be in the making. *Always use the* **unget** *command to cancel a* **get -e** *command.*

3. The absence of the branch flag in the flag table does not prevent the creation of all branches. It only prevents the **-b** option from creating a branch from a leaf delta. If a **get -e** is executed on any delta that is not a leaf delta, then a branch will be created. If the joint edit flag has been set, then the presence of a delta SID in the **p-file** for a direct descendant from the retrieved leaf delta will also cause a branch delta to be created.

4. There seems to be a minor bug involving the joint edit flag. The problem will occur when the mode of the directory is either 770 or 777 and joint edit is performed by two different users belonging to the same group. When a **get -e** is executed, the owner of the file is the ID of the effective user, which, in this case, is the same as the real user. When the second user attempts a **get -e**, the command will fail with the following message:

ERROR [s.xx.c]: 'p.xx.c' unreadable or unwritable (ut7)

However, the **get** command will have changed the name of the owner of the **p-file** to the ID of the effective user that executed the command. If the command is executed again by the second user, it will succeed. If the procedures outlined in Chapter 10 and 11 are followed, the problem can be avoided. See those chapters for a detailed explanation.

CHAPTER 6

Updating
the SCCS File
The "delta" Command

6.1 Introduction

The **delta** command is the only way to add a new delta to an SCCS file. The basis of this new delta is the **g-file** and the **p-file** created by the **get** command. Since all the decisions about the future delta were made when the **get** command was executed, the **delta** command is very straightforward. With the **delta** command, we are limited to:

- Entering the Modification Request numbers
- Entering delta comments
- Keeping the **g-file**
- Specifying which delta SID to use
- Suppressing the delta summary information
- Printing the delta

6.2 Command Syntax

The format for the **delta** command is as follows:

```
delta [-y{comment}] [-m{mrlist}] [-n] [-r{SID}] [-s]
[-p] [-g{ignore list}] {file . . .}
```

The next section discusses a simple delta with no options. The subsequent sections are organized to discuss the various options in logical groupings. Each group will show how the default action of the **delta** command can be modified to produce different results.

6.3 No Options: The Default Parameters

The simplest form of the command is

delta {file . . .}

where the variable {**file . . .**} follows the rules for file names discussed in Section 2.4. The file name is the SCCS file name and **not** the name of the **g-file**. This requires that the **g-file** be present in the current working directory and that it must have a name that is the same as that of the SCCS file without the "s." prefix. The SCCS file may exist in another directory. In fact, as we shall see in Chapter 11, it is a bad practice to edit a file in the same directory as the SCCS file.

Anytime a delta is made, a comment as to the reason for making the delta must be entered. In the above form of the **delta** command, the comment must be entered via the standard input. If the standard input has not been redirected from the terminal, then the prompt **comments?** is printed on standard output. Whether the standard input has been redirected or not, the standard input is read for a comment that may contain any arbitrary text.* When entered from the standard input, a newline character will terminate the text. If newlines are to be a part of the text, they must be escaped with a "\". Although it is not recommended practice, a null string is considered a valid comment. The following are a few examples of valid ways to enter comments:

> **$ delta s.exampl.c**
> comments? **A single line comment**

> **$ delta s.exampl.c**
> comments? **A multiline comment** \
> **would look like this**

It should be noted that the multiple-line comment shown in the last example will result in a separate delta comment record being created for each line of text.

If the **v** flag has been set for the SCCS file (see the delta command parameter discussion in Chapter 4), then the **delta** command will also prompt for modification request numbers. If standard input has not been redirected, then the prompt **MRs?** will precede the **comments?** prompt. The rules for MR numbers are the same as the rules for entering comments. Entering MRs and comments would be similar to the following examples:

---

* Some systems limit the length of the text to 512 characters

> **$ delta s.exampl.c**
> MRs? **mr1 mr2**
> comments? **Single line MR numbers**
>
> **$ delta s.exampl.c**
> MRs? **mr1** \
> **mr2**
> comments? **Multiple lines for MR numbers**

Both of the above examples will produce a record for each MR number entered. It does not make any difference whether all the MRs are entered on one line or separate lines. The only requirement is that each number be separated from the next by a space or a tab character.

Prior to performing the delta operation, the **delta** command checks the following items:

1. That a valid **g-file** exists for the named SCCS file.
2. That a valid **p-file** exists for the named SCCS file.
3. That a record exists in the **p-file** for the user's login name. If more than one record exists with the same login name, then the **-r** option must be used to define which delta SID is correct.
4. The same permission checks performed for the **-e** option of the **get** command (see Chapter 5) are performed here.
5. If MR numbers are provided and the program name argument to the **v** flag exists in the SCCS file, then the MR numbers are passed to the named program for validation. A nonzero return indicates that the numbers were invalid. Appendix D provides information on how to implement an MR number validation program.

If all validation checks are passed, then **delta** retrieves the original source file based on the information in the **p-file** and writes this source to the **d-file**. The **g-file** and the **d-file** are compared by using the **bdiff** command. The resulting delta is merged with the existing SCCS file to create a new SCCS file called the **x-file**. As a final step, **delta** removes the old SCCS file and renames the **x-file** to the name of the SCCS file.

Note: The use of the **x-file** is why SCCS files cannot be linked to any other file names since the link would be broken everytime the old SCCS file was removed.

At the completion of the delta, the following messages will be printed on the standard output:

[**<File Name>**]   (Printed for multiple files)
<SID of Delta>
<Number of Lines Inserted> **inserted**
<Number of Lines Deleted> **deleted**
<Number of Lines Unchanged> **unchanged**
[**<error messages>**]

For example, in response to any of the above examples, the following might be printed:

```
3.4
4 inserted
2 deleted
35 unchanged
```

Remember that SCCS only supports two types of edits, insert and delete. Thus, if a line was changed, it would count as 1 delete and 1 insert. As a result, the line count does not reflect the actual changes made to the file but, rather, the edit control records generated for SCCS to re-create the file.

If no ID keywords are found in the source file, the message "No id keywords" is printed as an error message. This is a warning message unless the **i** flag was set in the SCCS file (see Chapter 4 for details).

6.4 Comments and MR Numbers

By using the **-y** option, comments can be entered as part of the command line, and the **delta** command will not prompt for any comments. Since a newline is no longer used to terminate the comment text, any comment including space or tabs must be enclosed in quotes. However, newlines are permissible as long as the comment string is enclosed in single quotes. The following are examples of a single-word comment, single-line comment, and multiple-line comment:

```
$ delta -yword s.exampl.c
$ delta -y"A single line" s.exampl.c
$ delta -y'A multiple
> line comment' s.exampl.c
```

Just as comments can be entered on the command line, the **-m** option provides the same capability for MR numbers. The rules are the same as for comments. Combining the two options gives the following command:

```
$ delta -y"a comment" -m"mr01 mr02" s.exampl.c
```

6.5 Saving the "g-file"

The **g-file** is normally deleted once the delta has been made. However, the **-n** option will force the **g-file** to be retained. Use of this option should be done with the realization that the ID keyword strings in the **g-file** have not been expanded.

Lack of the proper ID keyword strings will defeat the use of the **what** command in determining the SID of an object file. On the opposite side of the coin, doing a **delta** followed by a **get** will change the last modified time of the source file. If **make** is being used to build a product, this will cause **make** to view the file as newer than any target for which it is a dependency.

This option should be used only for testing. If editing of the source file is finished, it is better to execute a **delta** followed by a **get** and then to rebuild the product with the correct ID keyword strings.

6.6 Specifying Which Delta SID

This option is rarely used since, normally, a user only edits one copy of a source file at a time. However, in those rare instances where two different entries exist in the **p-file** for the same user, the **-r{SID}** option is used to select the correct SID for the delta. Notice that either the SID of the delta to be created or the SID retrieved can be used as the argument. Using Figure 5.1 as an example, if "pgmr1" performed the two commands

$$\text{\$ get -e s.exampl.c}$$
$$\text{\$ get -e -r1.3.1 s.exampl.c,}$$

the **p-file** would contain these entries:

```
3.2 3.3 pgmr1 88/10/20 20:08:34
1.3.1.3 1.3.1.4 pgmr1 88/10/20 21:14:23
```

To delta the change for the retrieved SID of 3.2, the command line would be entered as follows:

$$\text{\$ delta -r3.3 s.exampl.c}$$

While either SID may be used, use the delta SID instead of the retrieved SID. The reason is that if the joint edit flag were set for the SCCS file it would be possible to have the same retrieved SID appear more than once in the **p-file**. However, the delta SID will never have a duplicate since it is not possible to create duplicate SIDs to an SCCS File.

6.7 Suppressing Standard Output

The **-s** option suppresses the printing of the delta summary information (see above) on the standard output. It does not suppress the "comments?" and "MRs?" prompts. To suppress all printing to standard output, the **-y** and **-m** (if required) options must also be used.

Thus, assuming the **v** flag has been set, the command

$ delta -y"comment" -mmr01 -s s.exampl.c

will suppress all printing to standard output and will also suppress all input from standard input. This option is useful in shell scripts and/or in combination with the **-p** option, which is described in the next section.

6.8 Printing SCCS File Differences

The difference between the **g-file** and **d-file** can be printed to the standard output with the use of the **-p** option. The prompts and delta summary messages will be mixed with the report, unless this option is combined with the **-y**, **-m** (if required), and **-s** options. Thus, the command is as follows:

$ delta -p -y"comment" -mmr01 -s s.exampl.c

Figure 6.1 is an example of what this report would be like. As can be seen, this is the same as the output of **bdiff**.

```
3c3
< This is line 2; revision 0.
---
> This is line 2; revision 1.
5a6
> This is line 5; revision 1.
```

Figure 6.1 Difference Report from Delta -p Command

6.9 Ignoring a Previous Delta

The format for the option is

-g{ignore list},

where the argument {**ignore list**} has the same syntax as the argument {**include list**} for the **-i** option of the **get** command. The {**ignore list**} is a list of deltas to be ignored when the SCCS file is accessed using the SID created by this delta.

The above is what the manual says is the purpose of this option. However, after several tests, it seems that the @**g** record of the delta table is ignored by the **get** command. This is not a problem, because the same function can be performed by using the **-x** option of the **get** command.

6.10 Helpful Hints

1. If the standard input has been redirected by the use of a minus sign (-) for the file name argument, the **-y** option (and if the **v** flag is set, the **-m** option) must be used to enter comments and MR numbers. Failure to do this will result in the first one or two lines of standard input being used to answer the prompts for comments and MRs. Let's say the **v** flag has not been set. In this case, the first file name would become the comment used in all subsequent file names. Definitely, this is not the desired result. The correct format for the command is as follows:

<pre>
$ delta -y"comment line" -   (v flag not set)
$ delta -y"comment line" -mmr01 -   (v flag set)
</pre>

2. When {**file . . .**} specifies multiple files, the same comments and MR numbers are entered for all the files specified. Given this restriction, the specification of multiple files should only be done when the same change has been made to every source file. Also, in this situation, if MR numbers are entered, then every file must have the **v** flag set or the delta for that source file will be rejected.

3. Any file not retrieved with the **-k** or **-e** options of the **get** command will have the ID keywords replaced with actual values. This happens when a source file has been retrieved with the following command:

<pre>
$ get s.exampl.c
</pre>

Let's say that, after looking at the file, we decide that it needs to be changed. Instead of doing the proper thing and executing a **get-e**, the source file as retrieved with the above command is edited. A delta is then attempted and fails because there is no **p-file**. So, being in a bit of a hurry, the command

<pre>
$ get -g -e s.exampl.c
</pre>

is executed to create a **p-file** but suppress the creation of a **g- file**. When the delta is attempted again, the message "No id keywords" will be displayed. Why do we get this message? Because the source file that was edited had the ID keywords replaced with actual values, so the ID keywords no longer exist in the source file (see Chapter 8 for an explanation of ID keywords). There are two ways to fix this kind of error. If the number of changes is very small, it is easier to delete the delta with the **rmdel** command (see Chapter 7) and start from the beginning without using any shortcuts. However, if the number of changes is very large, getting out of it is going to be a lot more work. The following are the suggested steps to take to restore the ID keywords:

  a. Retrieve the source file but without the **-e** option otherwise, it will be impossible to delete the delta.
  b. Delete the delta with the **rmdel** command.

c. Change the file mode on the retrieved file and then edit the file to put back the ID keywords.

d. Execute the **get** command with the **-g** and **-e** options so that a **p-file** is created.

e. Delta the corrected version of the file.

CHAPTER 7

SCCS File
Maintenance

7.1 Introduction

In the last three chapters, we discussed how to create an SCCS file, retrieve a source file from an SCCS file, and store a source file in an SCCS file. While these three functions constitute the core of the activity surrounding SCCS files, we must also know how to accomplish the following:

- Make administrative changes to an SCCS file
- Correct delta comments of an SCCS file
- Correct modification request numbers
- Delete a leaf delta
- Combine deltas
- Fix SCCS file problems

These tasks are the topics for this chapter. By the end of this chapter, all the commands dealing with the creation and modification of an SCCS file will have been discussed.

7.2 Making Administrative Changes

In Chapter 4 we discussed the establishment of the initial values for each of the sections of an SCCS file. In Chapters 5 and 6 we saw how to make changes to the body of source and the delta table of an SCCS file. In this chapter we shall learn how to make changes to the user table, the flag table, and the descriptive text sections of the SCCS file. As with the initialization of an SCCS file, the command used to perform these functions is the **admin** command.

7.2.1 "admin" Command Syntax for SCCS File Modification

The following format for the **admin** command only covers those options that are related to modifying an SCCS file:

> **admin [-a{login name | numerical group ID}]**
> **[-e{login name | numerical group ID}]**
> **[-f{flag}[{flag-val}]]**
> **[-d{flag} | -dl{list}]**
> **[-t[{text file}]] {file . . .}**

The following sections are organized to discuss the above options by groups, according to the section of the SCCS file that is being modified. The argument **{file . . .}** follows the rules for SCCS file names discussed in Section 2.4.

7.2.2 Changing the User Table

Section 4.5 discussed how to add login names or group IDs to the user table using the **-a** option. Just as names can be added to the user table, names can be deleted from the table through the use of the **-e** option. The syntax and rules for the **-e** option are the same as those for the **-a** option, and one or more **-a** and/or **-e** options can appear on the same command line. For example, the command

$ admin -ageorge -e!joe -e104 s.exampl.c

will add "george" to the list of valid users and would delete "!joe" and group ID "104" from the list of valid users.

Note: To erase a user or group, the argument for the **-e** option must be identical to the entry in the user table.

Thus, a user that has been denied permission (login name or numerical group ID prefixed by a "!") must be entered with the "!" prefix.

Warning! If the argument to the **-e** option specifies a nonexistent entry, no warning or error message will be given telling you that the entry was not found. So watch out for typing errors.

7.2.3 Changing the Flag Table

Each flag described in Appendix A is set with the **-f** option (used in Chapter 4 for the initial flag settings) and turned off with the **-d** option. The term *setting a flag* with the **-f** option means that a record for that flag is added to the flag table. To turn off a flag, the record has to be deleted with the **-d** option. Except for the lock (**l**) flag, none of the flags require any arguments when using the **-d** option.

With the exception of a few flags, the majority of the flags have already been discussed in Chapter 4. The following sections are divided according to the different categories of flags as shown in Table 4.1. In each category, those flags that had previously been skipped (because they applied to active files) will now be discussed. In addition, any comments regarding the effects of changing a flag from its initial value will be made.

Delta access flags.   The category of flags called *delta access flags* includes all those flags that limit which deltas can be *retrieved for editing*. Any delta of an SCCS file can always be retrieved, and the default is to allow any delta to be retrieved for editing (the **-e** option of the **get** command). SCCS provides three ways to lock out all deltas of a release (SIDs that have the same release number, **R**) from being retrieved for editing. These are as follows:

1. A floor can be defined that will prevent all SIDs with a release number less than the floor from being retrieved for editing. The default value for the floor is 1, although it can be any number that is greater than 0 or less than 9999. To set the floor, the **f{floor}** flag is used. For example, the command

   $ admin -ff3 s.exampl.c

   will lock all release numbers that are less than 3 from being retrieved for editing. If the branch flag has been set, then all branches with release numbers that are less than the floor will also be locked. To restore the floor to the default value, the command

   $ admin -df s.exampl.c

   is used. If you were to look at the SCCS file, you would find that the **-d** option deleted the floor record from the flag table.

2. Just as a floor can be set, a ceiling can be set, which is the highest release number than can be retrieved for editing. The default value for the ceiling is 9999. By the use of the **c{ceil}** flag, the ceiling can be set to any number that is greater than 0 and less than or equal to 9999. The ceiling can be used to prevent any accidental changes to the release number. Using Figure 5.1 as an example, the following **get** command would force a new release number to be created:

   $ get -e -r4 s.exampl.c

To prevent this from accidentally happening, use the following command to set the ceiling:

$ admin -fc3 s.exampl.c

This says that the highest release number that can be retrieved for editing is 3. Later, when further development is OK, the ceiling could be deleted with the command

$ admin -dc s.exampl.c

3. Another way is to lock a specific release or range of releases by using the l{**list**} flag. The argument {**list**} has the following syntax:

{**list**} = {**Release Number**}[, . . .] | **a**

where an "**a**" means all release numbers. The following examples show how to lock a single release, several releases, or all releases:

$ admin -fl2 s.exampl.c	(locks R = 2)
$ admin -fl2,4 s.exampl.c	(locks R = 2 and 4)
$ admin -fla s.exampl.c	(locks all releases)

While the normal **-d** option would delete the entire lock record from the flag table, the lock flag allows individual release numbers to be unlocked through use of the **-dl**{**list**} option. The syntax for {**list**} is the same as above. Thus, if multiple release numbers had been locked, it would be possible to unlock only one of them by use of the following command:

$ admin -dl2 s.exampl.c

> **Warning!** When all releases have been locked by the "a" argument to {list}, it is not possible to selectively unlock releases. Also, the **admin** command does not verify that the release numbers to be locked actually exist in the SCCS file. Nor does it issue any message when the -dl{list} specifies release numbers that have never been locked.

What if a single delta needs to be locked? Sorry, SCCS does not provide for this situation. The only choice is to lock out an entire release number using any one of the above options.

Delta creation flags.   Both the branch flag (**b**) and the null delta flag (**n**) were fully described in Chapter 4. Both flags can be set or deleted at any time without creating any adverse impact on the SCCS file. It does not create a problem even when the branch flag is deleted and there is an outstanding delta SID for a branch delta in the **p-file**. The branch flag only affects the ability to force the creation of a branch from a leaf delta without having to first create a direct descendant. It has no effect on the ability to create a direct descendant from any leaf delta on a branch.

Get command parameters.   As was stated in Chapter 5, when a file is retrieved, the default SID is **mR.mL**. The **d{SID}** flag can be used to change this default to any valid value of **R**, **R.L**, **R.L.B**, or **R.L.B.S** (for more information, see the **-r** option of the **get** command). Using Figure 5.1 as an example, the command

$ admin -fd1.3.1 s.exampl.c

will set the default SID to be retrieved to 1.3.1.mS.

To set the default SID back to **mR.mL**, the default SID flag can be deleted as shown in the following example:

$ admin -dd s.exampl.c

Changing the default SID has to be done with full understanding of the delta SID that will be created when a file is retrieved for editing. In fact, why change the default SID from **mR.mL**? One possibility is when a particular branch is to be retrieved by default. In this situation, the default SID would be set to **R.L.B** and the default SID retrieved would then be **R.L.B.mS**. Another use is to force the change to a new release number. However, this use also shows the dangers of setting a new default SID.

Since the default SID only applies when no SID has been specified on the **get** command line (see Section 5.4.1), there is a hidden danger in using the flag to force a new release. If the joint edit flag has also been set, it is possible to create a technically illegal situation in the SCCS file. For example, if pgmr1 executed the command

$ get -e s.exampl.c,

the delta SID would be 4.1. Right after this, pgmr2 executes the following command:

$ get -e -r3.2 s.exampl.c

Instead of creating a branch delta SID, the delta SID for the last command would be 3.3. The problem is that the last delta SID is not part of the progeny of SID 4.1, even though the naming conventions imply otherwise. That's the bad news. The good news is that SCCS does not allow this error to be carried forward into future generations. Even if the **d** flag is turned off, the default SID retrieved would be 4.1.

Note that the **admin** command does not check the validity of the SID entered with the **d** flag. If it is not a valid SID, the error will not be discovered until the **get** command is used without any options that affect the SID retrieved.

Keyword definition flags.   Since the **m**, **q**, and **t** flags only change informational variables in the flag table, they can be added, deleted, or changed without affecting the use of the SCCS file. However, such is not the case with the **i** flag.

Without an Id keyword string argument, the **i** flag can be set or deleted at any time. The potential problem arises when the ID keyword string is given as an argument. If deltas have already been made to the SCCS file and the validation string is different than the ID keyword strings in prior deltas, there will be a problem in retrieving old deltas. The **get** command will fail because the validation string does not match the ID keyword string retrieved. The only known solution to this problem is to delete the **i** flag.

Given the above limitation to change, either do not use the ID keyword validation string or consider one of the following options:

1. Set the **i** flag with the ID keyword validation string when the SCCS file is created. Once it is set, consider it to be carved in stone and never change it.
2. The same as item 1, except the ID keyword string would be defined as "**%W%**". This string is the minimal string used in the source file and is the only string defined by the **i** flag. If necessary, a different string can be substituted when the file is retrieved by using the **-w** option of the **get** command.

The joint edit flag (**j**) was fully discussed in Chapter 4 and can be changed at any time without affecting on the SCCS file.

Delta command parameters.   The **v** flag can be changed at any time. Just remember that once turned off the **-m** option can no longer be given on the command line without producing an error.

7.2.4 Changing the Descriptive Text

To change the descriptive text, the command format is the same as for adding descriptive text (see Chapter 4). The text contained in the file specified by {**text file**} will replace any existing descriptive text. To delete all descriptive text from the SCCS file, use the **-t** option without any argument.

For example, the command

$ admin -tsample.txt s.exampl.c

will replace any existing text with the new text contained in the file **sample.txt**.
While the command

$ admin -t s.exampl.c

will delete any existing descriptive text.

7.3 Making Changes to Deltas

There are three commands for altering delta information in an SCCS file. The
commands are as follows:

- The **cdc** command to change the delta commentary
- The **comb** command to combine several deltas into one delta
- The **rmdel** command to remove the last delta made

As will be seen in the following sections, these commands are very limited in what
functions they can perform.

7.3.1 Changing the Commentary for a Delta

The **cdc** command is used to change the comment and/or MR records in the specified
delta. While the **cdc** command can be used to correct entries made in error, it is
also useful for adding notes to existing deltas.

Syntax for the "cdc" command.   The syntax for the **cdc** command is as
follows:

cdc -r{SID} [-y[{comment}]] [-m[{mrlist}]] {files . . .}

The following section discusses the **cdc** command with no options so that the
default action is understood. Then we will discuss how to use the options to modify
the default action of the command.

Default parameters for the "cdc" command.   The basic form of the command is

cdc -r{SID} {files . . .}

where the argument {**files . . .**} follows the rules for SCCS file names discussed in

Section 2.4. Note, if the minus sign (-) is used as a file name, the standard input is read for a list of file names. With the standard input being used for file names, the **-y** option and, if the **v** flag is set, the **-m** option must be a part of the command line.

The **-r{SID}** must be a part of the command line and must be a specific SID (**R.L** or **R.L.B.S**) and it must exist in the SCCS file. There is no default SID, and ambiguous SIDs are considered to be nonexistent.

If the **v** flag is set for the SCCS file and the standard input is the terminal, then the prompt **MRs?** will be printed on the standard output. If the standard input is not the terminal, no prompt is issued. To add an MR number, the syntax is the same as for the **delta** command (see Chapter 6). An MR number may also be deleted by prefixing the MR number with the character **!**. The list of MR numbers deleted is changed into a "comment" line and added to the delta table as a comment record. If the MR numbers are not to be changed, then enter a <newline> with no other information. For the **cdc** command, a null entry means ignore the option.

After any MR number changes have been entered, changes to the delta comments will be solicited. If the standard input is a terminal, then the prompt **comments?** will be printed on the standard output. As with the above, no prompt is issued when the standard input is not a terminal. The rules for entry of comments are the same as those for the **delta** command (see Chapter 6). Any entry, other than a null entry, becomes the first comment record for the delta. Any previous comments are marked as having been changed.

Figure 7.1 shows the delta entry prior to changing the delta commentary with the following command (assuming the **v** flag is set):

```
$ cdc -r1.1 s.exampl.c
MRs? !mr001 mr002 mr003
comments? additional comments
```

```
 .
 .
 .
@s 00043/00000/00000
@d D 1.1 89/02/12 16:12:15 pgmr1 1 0
@m mr001
@c Example 1
@e
 .
 .
 .
```

Figure 7.1   Original Delta Entry

The revised delta entry is shown in Figure 7.2.

```
        .
        .
        .
   @s 00043/00000/00000
   @d D 1.1 89/02/12 16:12:25 pgmr1 1 0
   @m mr002
   @m mr003
   @c additional comments
   @c *** LIST OF DELETED MRS ***
   @c mr001
   @c *** CHANGED *** 89/02/12 17:03:01 pgmr1
   @c Example 1
   @e
        .
        .
        .
```

Figure 7.2 Delta Entry Modified by cdc Command

Note that not everyone can change the delta commentary. First, the effective user ID must have write permission in the SCCS file directory. In addition, only the owner of the SCCS file or the user who made the delta can make a change. For this purpose, the test is based on the real user ID and not the effective user ID.

Since the SCCS file is being modified, a **z-file** (see Chapter 5) is created to prevent anyone else from changing the file. If the **v** flag is set and an MR validation program name given, the MR numbers are then passed to the validation program. A nonzero return from the validation program will cause **cdc** to abort. The revised SCCS file is written to the **x-file**, which is renamed when processing is complete.

Changing the default parameters.   The **-y** and **-m** options function the same as the corresponding options in the **delta** command. The one difference is that a null entry means ignore the option. This is important when the **v** flag is set for the SCCS file, as shown in the following examples.

To change the comments for SID 1.3, the command is as follows:

$ **cdc -r1.3 -y"new comment line" -m s.exampl.c**

If the **-m** option had not been entered on the command line and the **v** flag was set, then the **cdc** command would have prompted for the MR numbers. The reverse is also true; if only the MR numbers needed to be modified, the following command is used:

$ cdc -r1.3 -y -m"!mr01 mr03" s.exampl.c

7.3.2 Combining Deltas

Each delta made to an SCCS file causes the file to get larger and larger. At a minimum, every delta adds another set of records to the delta table. Whether text is being added, deleted, or changed, the body of the SCCS file will reflect those changes in edit control records and text records. Even a delta that deletes the entire source file would increase the size of the body of the SCCS file by the two control records required to define the beginning and end of the portion to be deleted. When many deltas have been performed, this may have a significant impact on the size of the SCCS file and on the time it takes to retrieve a source file from the SCCS file. The **comb** command is therefore used to consolidate deltas, which may result in a smaller SCCS file and improved retrieval time. As will be seen, there are a few cases where the SCCS file may be larger after consolidation.

Syntax for the "comb" command.   The syntax for the **comb** command is as follows:

comb [-s] [-c{preserve list}] [-p{SID}] [-o] {files . . .}

As with other commands, the following section will look at the default operation of the command. Then we will show how to print a summary report and alternative methods for defining the structure of the resultant delta tree. Finally, a few helpful hints are provided.

"comb" command with no options.   The basic command format is

comb {files . . .}

where the argument {**files . . .**} follows the rules for SCCS file names discussed in Section 2.4.

When no options are given, the minimal number of deltas is preserved. For a delta to be preserved, it must meet one of the following conditions:

1. The delta is the leaf delta of either the trunk or a branch. A leaf delta meets the condition of **mR.mL** or, for each branch, **R.L.B.mS**.
2. The delta is an ancestor delta that is required to preserve the shape of the SCCS tree. Thus, every delta that forms the juncture of a new branch must be kept.

Using Figure 5.1 as the starting SCCS delta tree, the **comb** command would only keep deltas 1.3, 1.3.1.3, and 3.2. The revised tree is shown in Figure 7.3. This tree preserves the shape of the delta tree and has a minimal number of deltas. In addition to dropping nonessential deltas, **comb** makes the following changes to the SCCS file:

1. The comments and MR numbers of all the original deltas are preserved in the descriptive text segment of the SCCS file.
2. The initial delta in the new SCCS file is established with a null record for MRs, and the original comment is replaced with "This was COMBined"
3. As shown in Figure 5.3, the SIDs for the leaf deltas have new names.

The **comb** command does not actually perform the compression of the SCCS file. It generates a shell procedure, which it writes to the standard output. This shell procedure must then be executed in order to actually compress the SCCS file. The sequence of commands is as follows:

```
$ comb s.exampl.c > shrink
$ sh shrink
$ rm shrink
```

As we shall see later, it may be necessary to make some minor adjustments to the shell script for it to execute properly.

Options to the "comb" command.   Before combining deltas in an SCCS file, it would be nice to know if it is worth the effort. The **-s** option will solve this problem by changing the generated shell script to one that will produce a summary report. This report gives the file name, percentage of change, size (in blocks) after combining deltas, and size (in blocks) before combining deltas. Thus, the command sequence

```
$ comb -s s.exampl.c > shrink
$ sh shrink
```

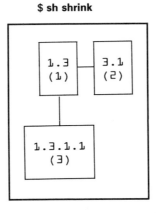

Note: The numbers in parentheses are the delta sequence numbers.

Figure 7.3 SID Chart for COMBined SCCS File

might generate a report that looks like the following:

s.exampl.c 50%　10/20

Should the default rules for generating a new delta tree not produce the desired results, the **comb** command provides three alternative options for building a new delta tree. While the **comb** command does not prevent them from being on the same command line, each option follows different rules. Should they be combined, the generated shell script may not execute.

The first option to be discussed is the **-p{SID}** option. This option drops all deltas prior to the specified {SID}. Using Figure 5.1 as an example, let's say that anything prior to release 3.1 is ancient history and is no longer needed for any purpose and should therefore be combined. To accomplish this objective, the following command is used:

```
$ comb -p3.1 s.exampl.c > shrink
$ sh shrink
```

The resulting delta tree is as shown in Figure 7.4. Why is the tree shaped this way? To understand how the **-p** option works, translate the {SID} into a delta sequence number. Every SID with a delta sequence number less than the specified SID is dropped. And there is no rule that says the {SID} has to be a trunk SID. The trap with this option is that it cannot only radically change the shape of the tree, but it can also eliminate leaf deltas. Consider the **-p** option to be a saw that

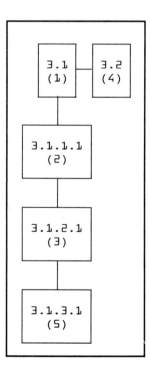

Note: The numbers in parentheses are the delta sequence numbers.

Figure 7.4　SID Chart from Use of -p Option

cuts off a tree at a certain point. Any unattached branches are grafted back onto the trunk at the base.

As a general rule, the **-p** option should not be used on delta trees that have branches.

Given a delta tree with no branches, the default would have been to create a tree with one delta. This may be a bit too radical. Instead, the **-p** option can be used to eliminate the oldest part of the tree and still preserve all the current deltas.

In the default option, the minimal number of deltas are preserved, the shape of the tree is maintained, and the sequence of the deltas is maintained. The **-o** option changes the rules so that the emphasis is on preserving the minimal number of leaves. The rule is that there will be no more than one leaf per release number. Furthermore, the latest delta for a particular release number will become the leaf delta.

Due to the structure of the tree in Figure 5.1, the tree generated by the **-o** option is the same as the default. However, what happens if there is a branch named 3.1.1.1 with a delta sequence number of 9. The default is to keep it as a separate branch. Using the **-o** option, the name would be changed to 3.3. Delta 3.2 is not dropped; it is just no longer the leaf delta. Obviously, the **-o** option can have a rather dramatic impact on the shape of the delta tree.

For the above options as well as the default, the **comb** command provides the rules for generating a new source tree. With the **-c** option, the delta tree is built based on the information provided in the {**preserve list**}. In the "define your own tree" game, the rules are as follows:

1. The list of deltas is very important because only the deltas specified in the list are preserved.
2. The first delta specified becomes the base of the tree. Thus, to avoid problems, do not make a branch delta the first delta.
3. Finally, to create a branch, a direct descendant must first be defined.

For example, the command

$ comb -c1.3,1.3.1.3,3.2 s.exampl.c > shrink

makes 1.3.1.3 become the direct descendant of 1.3 instead of being a branch. To create the delta tree shown in Figure 7.3, the following command sequence is used:

$ comb -c1.3,3.2,1.3.1.3 s.exampl.c > shrink
$ sh shrink

Warning! When more than one SCCS file is given, each option must apply to every file to be processed. If they do not, the **comb** command will abort when it finds an error.

Helpful hints for the "comb" command

1. If the generated shell script fails because a comb$$ (where $$ is the process number) script cannot be found, check the PATH environmental variable. The generated shell scripts assume that the current directory is part of the search path.

2. The **-p**, **-o**, and **-c** options must never be combined. Each has its own separate and distinct rules for building a tree, and these rules are not compatible.

3. As of this writing, the generated shell script has problems with flag table variables that include spaces or tabs. It fails to enclose these variables in quotation marks. As a result, the shell script will fail because the additional variables are treated as file names. The problem can be overcome by editing the shell script to put in the missing quotation marks.

4. Always check the SCCS file by using the **-s** option before actually executing the **comb** command. You may find that there is little or no savings in space to be gained.

5. If space savings is an important factor, there is a way to reduce the size of the files. All the old delta history is maintained in the descriptive text segment. To preserve the history, use the **prs** command (see Chapter 8) to print the descriptive text segment. The **admin** command can then be used to delete the descriptive text (see above).

6. The **comb** command should be used on an exception basis, rather than as a scheduled procedure. Part of the price paid in every consolidation is a loss of the detailed changes that made up each delta. This limits the ability to include, exclude or create branches based on specific changes.

7. Always backup the SCCS files before using the **comb** command. Occasionally, the **comb** command will not work properly and the resulting SCCS file will not be usable. With a backup, you can at least return to where you started.

7.3.3 Removing Deltas

Every now and then, a delta is made that should not have been made. The question is how to delete the delta from the SCCS file. If the delta is the most recent delta on the trunk or branch (a leaf delta), then the **rmdel** command can be used. The command syntax is simply

rmdel -r{SID} {files . . .}

where the argument **{files . . .}** follows the rules for SCCS files set forth in Section 2.4. The **{SID}** must be of the format **R.L** or **R.L.B.S.** If the specific SID is not known, the **get** command can be used to identify the SID of the leaf delta.

For example, the following command would delete delta 1.3.1.3 of Figure 5.1:

$ rmdel -r`get -r1 -t -g s.exampl.c `s.exampl.c

Before deleting a delta, the **rmdel** command checks the following:

1. If a **p-file** exists for the named SCCS file, it verifies that the delta being deleted has not been retrieved for edit.
2. That the real user ID of the person deleting the delta is the same as the login name of the person who made the delta, or is the same as that of the owner of the SCCS file.
3. That the effective user ID has write permission in the directory.

Since the SCCS file is being modified, a **z-file** is created to prevent access by any other SCCS command. The revised SCCS file is written to an **x-file**, which, upon successful completion of the delete, is renamed to the name of the SCCS file.

What happens if the delta to be deleted has descendants or has been retrieved for edit. In the first case, for every branch, including the trunk, in which that delta is an ancestor, the leaf delta needs to be retrieved for edit using the exclude option and then deltaed without making any other changes. Using Figure 5.1 as an example, we discover that delta 1.2 was absolutely wrong. The following series of commands removes it from all existing branches:

$ get -e -r3 -x1.2 s.exampl.c
$ delta s.exampl.c
$ get -e -r1.3.1 -x1.2 s.exampl.c
$ delta s.exampl.c

The problem is that without rebuilding the delta tree there is no way to prevent the bad SID from being retrieved for edit or from being included with another SID. The only thing that can be done is to lock out an entire release with either the floor or lock flags (see above).

If the delta has been retrieved for editing, there are two options. If the number of changes is not large, then the best solution is to use the **unget** command to cancel the **get-e** and then use the **rmdel** command to delete the delta. When this is not possible, the source file can be deltaed and then, following the sequence described above, we delete the unwanted delta.

7.4 Fixing SCCS File Problems

This is the disaster repair section. The methods discussed in this section are to be used when no SCCS command can be used to fix the problem and restoring the file from backup is not a viable solution. Some of the problems that can get you into this predicament are as follows:

1. Some unknown gremlin kicked a few bits around. As a result, the file has become corrupted. Furthermore, the SCCS file has not been accessed for a long time and all the backups made of the SCCS file have the same problem.
2. Somebody deltaed a file in which the last record is missing a line feed. The delta worked fine, but **get** refuses to retrieve the file. This problem usually occurs when converting source files from other systems.

7.4.1 Editing the SCCS File

First, you have to prevent anyone from touching the file while you are making changes. The one way that is recognized by all SCCS commands is to create a **z-file** that contains the process number of the command locking the file; any positive number will do. Just remember, the file name of the **z-file** is the SCCS file name with the "**s.**" changed to a "**z.**", and the file mode is 444.

Next, copy the SCCS file to the **x-file** (SCCS file name with the "**s.**" changed to an "**x.**"). After all, if you make a mistake you don't want to destroy your only copy even if it has a few problems.

Now the file can be fixed by editing the file with a suitable editor, such as **ed** or **vi**. As mentioned in Chapter 3, all SCCS control records begin with a control-A. Modifying a control record has to be done with extreme care. This is especially true of records in the delta table and the body of the SCCS file. Also, changing source file lines in the body of the SCCS file is one thing, but adding or deleting lines can cause all sorts of problems. Unless you fully understand how SCCS maintains the edit control lines, *don't modify them*!

When all the necessary changes have been completed, the **x-file** can be re-named to the name of the SCCS file and the **z-file** removed. However, before the file can be used, the checksum has to be fixed, as described in the following section.

7.4.2 Fixing the Checksum

If the checksum record is not correct, the SCCS commands will abort with a "corrupted file (co6)" message. To correct the checksum, the **-z** option of the **admin** command is used. When using the **-z** option, no other options are to be specified. The format for the command then is

admin -z {file . . .}

where the argument {**files . . .**} follows the rules for SCCS file names defined in Section 2.4.

As mentioned above, SCCS files can go for a long period of time without being accessed. To verify that the SCCS files have not become corrupted, the checksum should be checked on a regular basis with the **admin** command shown below:

admin -h {file . . .}

CHAPTER 8

How to Use
SCCS Information

8.1 Introduction

This chapter will discuss how to extract information contained in the SCCS file for the following purposes:

- Source file identification (ID keywords)
- Reports (Data keywords)

First, we shall consider how SCCS information can be embedded in the source file by use of the ID keywords, which provide the link between the source file and the SCCS file. Without them, identification of the delta that created a particular version of a source file would be very difficult. Next we shall discuss how, with the exception of the checksum record (which is only useful within SCCS), all the SCCS file information can also be displayed by using the data keywords of the **prs** command, the "Report Writer" for SCCS.

8.2 Embedding SCCS Information in the Source File

IDentification **keywords** is the name for a group of variables that can be placed in a source file (see Appendix B for the list of ID keywords). When the source file is retrieved via the **get** command and the **-e** or **-k** option is not used, the ID keywords are replaced with the appropriate information. These ID keywords can be used as source file comments and, if desired, can be formatted to be displayed by the **what** command (see below). As previously discussed, if the ID keywords are not present in a source file, any attempt to retrieve or delta such a source file will result in the "No id keywords" message being displayed. This message is a warning, except when the **i** flag is set, in which case it becomes a fatal error.

The large number of ID keywords shown in Appendix B is somewhat deceiving since many are variations of one element of data (for example, dates or file names) or are composites of several ID keywords (**%I%, %W%, or %A%**). In actuality, there are ID keywords for the SID or its components, the file name, current date and time, retrieved delta creation date and time, and the **m** flag, **q** flag, and **t** flag. While limited, this is sufficient information to provide the necessary SCCS file link to the source file.

To keep the shell, make, troff, 'C' compiler, or other compiler or text formatter from trying to process the ID keywords as commands, they have to be included in the source file as a comment or as a value to variable. To understand this, let's start with the following line being in the source file exampl.c:

%Z%Module Name: %M% Version: %I% Date: %D%

If the source file is retrieved with either a **get -e** or **get -k** command, the line will not change. However, with any other form of the **get** command, the variables will be replaced with the corresponding information when the file is retrieved. Note that the command **get -w** provides for a variation on this theme (see Chapter 5 for details). Using Figure 5.1, if the command

$ get -r1.3.1 s.exampl.c

is executed, the variables are substituted and the line looks like the following:

@(#)Module Name: exampl.c Version: 1.3.1.3 Date: 88/10/30

If the C compiler was trying to process this line, it would go crazy since it is not valid C syntax. The same is true if the above line was part of a shell script or part of a make file. To hide this line, it must take the form of either a comment or a variable as shown below:

A 'C' comment: /* %Z%Module Name: %M% Version: %I% Date: %D% */
A 'C' variable: char id[ ] = "%Z%Module Name: %M% Version: %I% Date: %D%";

From the above examples, several observations can be made:

1. Wherever they occur in the source file, the ID keywords will be substituted when the source file is retrieved. Thus, the ID keywords are *reserved words* and cannot be used as variable names within a source file.

2. For compiled programs, there is a difference between making the ID keywords

part of a comment or part of a variable. When the source file is compiled, the comments will be stripped and the resulting object file will not have an SCCS ID string. Whereas, if it is the value for a variable, it will then be passed through to the object file. This is important when the **what** command is to be used to identify object files. Just as ID keywords are the link between the SCCS file and the source file, they are also the link between the source file and the object file.

3. The above is a long version of an SCCS ID string. Using one of the composite ID keywords, it can be as short as the following:

    char id[ ] = "%A%";

    This is equivalent to the following line:

    char id[ ] = "%Z%%Y% %M% %I%%Z%";

4. The **%Z%** ID keyword forms the four-character sequence used by the **what** command as a tag to identify strings that it is to display.

It should be obvious that ID keywords serve a very important function and should be a part of every source file managed by SCCS. In fact, it should be the rule to have ID keyword strings in a source file, and not the exception. If you have doubts as to their importance, answer the question of how you can tell the difference between two versions of the same source file. If the answer is comments in the source file, then choose which is more reliable: (1) comments inserted by the person editing the source file (even at 3 in the morning); or (2) comments resulting from the expansion of ID keywords. From experience, we know that there is a big gap between the ideal—comments by authors of source files—and the reality.

Remember, ID keywords are not limited to being used by the **what** command. They can be used in source files for any purpose where identification of the source file is important. For example, the SID and date could be assigned to variables that are displayed as part of a menu system. Thus, the user can quickly identify the current version of the program he is running.

8.3 The "what" Command

The **what** command searches any file, whether it be a source file, data file, or object file, and displays to the standard output any string that begins with the tag **@(#)**. The string can be terminated with any of these characters: ~, >, \, newline, or a null character. The syntax for the command is

what [-s] {file . . .}

where the argument {**file . . .**} can be a single file, multiple files, or a directory.

While the most common use of the **what** command is in conjunction with SCCS to display the ID keyword strings, it is not limited to this function. A *what* *string* can be any string that is prefixed by the tag @(#). For example, a C program could contain the following lines:

char id1[ ] = "%W%";
char id2[ ] = "@(#)Product Information";

If a program containing these lines is to be compiled, then the command

$ what a.out

will print the following text:

```
a.out:
    exampl.c   1.3.1.3
    Product Information
```

This works well when a program consists of a single object module. However, most programs consist of many object modules resulting in a large amount of output from the **what** command. To make sense out of this mass of information, it should be prefixed with a header block. One way of doing this is to create a source file called pgmid.c, which would contain the lines

char id1[ ] = "%W% %D%";
char id2[ ] = "%Z%Product Information";
char id3[ ] = "%Z%Version status of the modules:";

For the %M% keyword to be the name of the program instead of pgmid.c (the default value for %M%), the **m** flag would be set with the value of "exampl". In addition, each source file that made up the program would contain the line:

char id[ ] = "%W%";

If the individual object modules were compiled and linked such that pgmid.o is always the first module, then the output will look like the following:

```
exampl:
    exampl   3.2 88/10/20
    Product Information
    Version status of the modules:
        mod1.c   1.2
        mod2.c   1.2
        mod3.c   3.2
```

If all the above information was not needed, then the **-s** option of the **what** command could be used to display only the first what string found in the file. For example, the command

$ what -s a.out

will display only the following line:

exampl:
exampl   3.2 88/10/20

What easier way can there be to identify the version of file, whether it be a source file or the final executable product?

8.4 "prs": The SCCS Report Writer

The **prs** command is a "Report Writer" in the most generic sense of the term. It is a window into the SCCS file through which every element of data from every section (except the checksum) can be extracted. Moreover, it can handle one delta or many deltas. The following are some of the tasks that can be performed using the **prs** command:

1. Quickly find out the basic information about any delta or group of deltas.
2. Prepare simple reports about an SCCS file or group of files.
3. Extract information for processing by other UNIX commands.

8.4.1 Syntax for the "prs" Command

The syntax for the **prs** command is as follows:

prs [-r[{SID}]] [-e] [-1] [-c{date-time}] [-a]
[-d{dataspec}] {file . . .}

The argument {**file . . .**} follows the rules for SCCS file names set forth in Section 2.4. The following section discusses the **prs** command when no options have been given. Following that, we shall see how we can control which deltas are selected. In the final section, we will discuss how to use data keywords to control the selection and formatting of the data items in an SCCS file.

8.4.2 Default Action for "prs" Command

Without any options, the format of the command is as follows:

prs {file . . .}

Since no SID is specified, **prs** will print to the standard output the contents of each active entry in the delta table. The order will be in the reverse order in which the deltas were created (descending delta sequence numbers) so that the most current delta is printed first. Using data keywords (see below) to identify the data items, the format for the information on each delta would be as follows:

```
                          <SCCS File Name>:

                          :Dt: :DL:
                          MRs:
                          :MR:
                          COMMENTS:
                          :C:
```

For a typical SCCS file, the output might look something like this:

```
        s.exampl.c

        D 1.2 88/10/21 14:30:23 ted 2 1 000008/000002/000014
        MRs:
        mr002
        mr003
        COMMENTS:
        modification comments for this delta

        D 1.1 88/09/11 10:15:48 ted 1 0 000014/000000/000000
        MRs:
        mr001
        COMMENTS:
        comments about the initial delta
```

8.4.3 Delta Selection for the "prs" Command

Instead of the entire active delta table, a single delta can be selected with the **-r[{SID}]** option. If the **{SID}** is not given, then the command

```
        $ prs -r s.exampl.c
```

will print the delta information in the format described above for the SID of **mR.mL**. To get information about a specific delta, the variable {SID} has to have the format of **R.L** or **R.L.B.S**. Thus, to obtain the delta information about SID 1.3.1.3, the command is

```
        $ prs -r1.3.1.3 s.exampl.c
```

When the {SID} is ambiguous (either **R** or **R.L.B**), the SID is resolved to either **R.mL** or **R.L.B.mS**. For example, the command

```
        $ prs -r3 s.exampl.c
```

will print the delta for SID 3.2.

The effect of the **-r{SID}** option can be expanded to select a range of deltas with either the **-e** or **-l** options. The **-e** option means to select the SID specified by the **-r** option plus all deltas with an earlier creation date. The **-l** is the same except that all deltas with a later creation date are added to the SID selected.

To get a better understanding of these options, lets look at what is happening from a different angle. The **-r** option specifies a delta by its SID. That delta also has a delta sequence number. From this point of view, we are starting at a specific delta sequence number. The **-e** option prints all deltas with a delta sequence number equal to or less than the delta sequence number selected. The **-l** option selects all deltas with a delta sequence number equal to or greater than the one selected. When branches exist in the SCCS file, this means that the deltas for all branches and the trunk are intermingled in the order of their creation.

For example, using Figure 5.1 as the delta tree, the command

$ prs -r3.1 -e s.exampl.c

will select deltas 3.1, 1.3, 1.2, and 1.1 in that order. Likewise, the command

$ prs -r3.1 -l s.exampl.c

will select deltas 1.3.1.3, 3.2, 1.3.1.2, 1.3.1.1, and 3.1 in that order.

Another way to specify the delta sequence number for the **-e** and **-l** options is to use the **-c{date-time}** option. The rules for entering the date and time are the same as for the **-c** option of the **get** command (see Chapter 5). This option must be combined with either the **-e** or **-l** options. For example, if delta information is needed on all deltas since 1/1/89, the following command is used:

$ prs -l -c890101000000 s.exampl.c

> Note that, had not the time been specified as 000000, it would have defaulted to 235959. This would have caused all deltas made on the specified day to be ignored.

In all the above, only the active deltas were selected. Deltas that had been deleted were ignored. To include deleted deltas in the list of selected deltas, the **-a** option must be used. The following are some examples of how to use the **-a** option:

$ prs -a s.exampl.c
$ prs -r3.1 -e -a s.exampl.c

Note that, if the last SID created has been deleted by the **rmdel** command, information about the SID can be displayed by using the **-a** option in combination with the **-r** option. The **prs** command line for this is as follows:

$ prs -r -a s.exampl.c

8.4.4 Defining Data Format for the "prs" Command

With the **-d**{**dataspec**} option, the output format of the data can be structured to extract any item of information, except for the checksum, from the SCCS file. The rules for the argument {**dataspec**} are as follows:

1. All data keywords defined in Appendix C can be used one or more times in a data specification. To make it easier to use, the appendix has been divided into sections that match the section of the SCCS file.
2. User text can be intermixed with data keywords. Just remember to be careful when using colons.
3. The tab and new-line characters are specified by $\backslash$**t** and $\backslash$**n**, respectively.
4. If the {dataspec} contains any white space, it must be enclosed in double quotes. For example, the command

   $ prs -r3.2 -d:Dt: s.exampl.c

   does not require quotes. However, the command

   $ prs -r -d"File: :F: Latest Delta :I:" s.exampl.c

   will have to be quoted.
5. Watch out for the data keywords that produce multiple lines of output (for example, :MR:, :C:, or :FL:). The **prs** command keeps multiple-line text as multiple lines. For example, each MR number will be separated by a newline character. Trying to construct readable reports under these circumstances can be a real challenge.
6. The default delta selected for the **-d** option is the delta with the highest delta sequence number. Using Figure 5.1 as the delta tree, the command

   $ prs -d:Dt: s.exampl.c

   will print the following line:

   D 1.3.1.3 89/02/06 18:04:06 pgmr1 8 6

7. To print the information for more than one delta, the **-e** or **-l** options must be used. For example, the command

   $ prs -e -d:Dt: s.exampl.c

   will print the entire delta table. Likewise, the command

   $ prs -e -d":F: :Dt:" s.exampl.c

will print the entire table with each line prefixed by the SCCS filename.

8. Have lots of patience. What you think your going to get is not always what you get!

The best way to understand the use of data keywords is with a few examples. The following examples show how to print data from each section of an SCCS file:

1. Previously, we saw how the **prs** command selects deltas in the order that they were created; this may not produce the most orderly report. However, with a minor change, a delta summary report with the SIDs in ascending order can be produced. The revised command line now reads as follows:

   $ prs -a -e -d:Dt: s.exampl.c | sort +1

   Using Figure 5.1 as an example, the **prs** command will print the following on the standard output:

   ```
   D 1.1 89/02/06 07:40:00 pgmr1 1 0
   D 1.2 89/02/06 08:13:00 pgmr1 2 1
   D 1.3 89/02/06 15:57:11 pgmr1 3 2
   D 1.3.1.1 89/02/06 18:00:04 pgmr1 5 3
   D 1.3.1.2 89/02/06 18:02:03 pgmr1 6 5
   D 1.3.1.3 89/02/06 18:04:32 pgmr1 8 6
   D 3.1 89/02/06 17:58:19 pgmr1 4 3
   D 3.2 89/02/06 18:03:14 pgmr1 7 4
   ```

2. The following command will print the contents of the user table:

   ```
   prs -d"User Table:\n:UN:" s.exampl.c
   User Table:
   pgmr1
   pgmr2
   !pgmr3
   ```

   > Note that, if information from the delta table is not being printed, then there is no need to use the **-r, -e, -l, -c,** or **-a** options.

3. The entire flag table can be printed with the following command:

   ```
   $ prs -d"Flag Table:\n:FL:" s.exampl.c
   branch
   id keywd err/warn
   ```

Individual flags can also be printed, as the following command shows:

$ prs -d"Branch: :BF:\nNull Delta: :ND:" \
> **s.exampl.c**
Branch: yes
Null Delta: no

Note that the difference in the output format between printing the entire
flag table and each individual flag. These differences are explained in
Appendix C.

---

4. There is only one data keyword for the descriptive section, so to print it you
might use the command

$ prs -d"File: :F: Descrip Text:\n:FD:" s.exampl.c

5. You could use the following command to retrieve a source file:

$ prs -r3.2 -d:GB: s.exampl.c

With the exception of an extra blank line at the end of the file, the above
command is equivalent to the **get** command

$ get -r3.2 s.exampl.c

whereas the command

$ prs -d:BD: s.exampl.c

will print the body of source exactly as it is in the SCCS file, including the
edit control records.

In the final analysis, the best way to understand the behavior of the **prs**
command is to use it. You will then begin to see which combinations work and
which produce alphabet soup. For example, the command

$ prs -r -d":Dt: :MR: :C:" s.exampl.c

works fine when there is only one MR number and one comment line. However,
if there are several MR numbers and several comment lines, the output becomes
rather difficult to read.

CHAPTER 9

Other
SCCS Commands

9.1 Introduction

There seems to be an unwritten law that states that in all attempts to separate items into categories there will always be a miscellaneous category. This chapter is the miscellaneous category for SCCS commands. As such, it contains the following commands:

- **sact:** print SCCS file editing activity
- **sccsdiff:** compare two versions of an SCCS file
- **val:** SCCS file validation checks
- **vc:** a macro preprocessor (UNIX System V).

Besides describing each command, suggestions on how the command can be used will also be given. This chapter is also the end of the discussion of the individual SCCS commands. Starting with Chapter 10, we put SCCS to work.

9.2 The "sact" Command

The **sact** command performs the following functions:

1. It is a quick way to determine which SCCS files have been retrieved with the **get-e** command. This is especially useful when you want to make sure that you have deltaed all the files that have been modified.

2. It can be used to print the contents of the **p-file**. Thus, for any SCCS file, we can know what SID has been retrieved and the delta SID to be created.

The format for this command is

sact {file . . .}

where the argument {**file . . .**} follows the rules for SCCS files defined in Section 2.4. Even though {**file . . .**} refers to the SCCS file name, the command is also looking for **p-file**s. For each **p-file** that matches the corresponding SCCS file defined by {**file . . .**}, **sact** will print on the standard output the contents of the **p-file** (see Chapter 5 for **p-file** record layout).

Assuming that there is a **p-file** for the SCCS File s.exampl.c, the command

$ sact s.exampl.c

will print the following on standard output:

3.2 3.3 ted 88/10/22 16:23:12

When multiple files or a directory is specified, the **sact** command will also print the name of the SCCS file before it prints the contents of the **p-file**.

9.3 The "sccsdiff" Command

Sometimes it is necessary to know the differences between any two versions of a source file. One way of doing this is to retrieve each version and then find the difference. Using Figure 5.1 as an example, the difference between version 1.2 and 3.1 could be obtained with the following sequence of commands:

```
$ get -k -r1.2 -p s.exampl.c > tmp1.c
$ get -k -r3.1 -p s.exampl.c > tmp2.c
$ bdiff tmp1.c tmp2.c
```

Instead of the above commands, the difference can also be obtained with the **sccsdiff** command, which has the following format:

sccsdiff -r{SID1} -r{SID2} [-p] [-s{n}] {file . . .}

The arguments {**SID1**} and {**SID2**} are the SIDs of the two deltas to be compared, and they must be in the form of **R.L** or **R.L.B.S**. The SIDs must exist as the **sccsdiff** command will complain bitterly about invalid, ambiguous, or nonexistent SIDs. If more than one file is named, the SIDs must exist in every file or **sccsdiff** will abort the first time it finds an invalid SID.

For the above example, the **sccsdiff** version of the command will be as follows:

$ sccsdiff -r1.2 -r3.1 s.exampl.c

The output can be made more elegant with the **-p** option, which pipes the output to the **pr** command. The **-p** option is equivalent to the following:

$ sccsdiff -r1.2 -r3.1 s.exampl.c | pr

The **sccsdiff** command does not actually compare the two versions of the source file. Instead, the file comparison is performed by the **bdiff** command. Occasionally, on a heavily loaded system, the **bdiff** command will fail because the default of 3,500 lines per segment that is passed to **diff** is too large. A smaller segment size can be specified with the **-s{n}** option, where {n} is the new segment size. As a point of information, the parameters are passed to the **bdiff** command in the following order:

bdiff <tmp1> <tmp2> {n}

The arguments <**tmp1**> and <**tmp2**> are the retrieved source files for the versions specified by {**SID1**} and {**SID2**}, respectively. So, be aware that the order in which the SIDs are specified is important because it affects the format of the final output.

9.4 The "val" Command

The **val** command performs up to six tests on a file of which four depend on the options given. These tests are as follows:

1. Is the file specified readable and is it an SCCS file?
2. Is the SCCS file corrupted?
3. Optionally, is the SID specified invalid or ambiguous?
4. Optionally, does the specified SID exist?
5. Optionally, does the module name match the argument specified in the **-m** option?
6. Optionally, does the module type match the argument specified in the **-y** option?

When you look at this list, the question arises, of what value is this command? All SCCS commands test for and ignore the files that do not meet the first test. They also check to see if the file is corrupted. Besides, the **admin -h** can be used to verify that the checksum is correct. In fact, all the tests can be performed just as easily by other commands. The answer is that, while the **val** command can be executed as a stand-alone command, its real value is when it is used in a shell program. To understand this value, let's see how it works.

The format for the **val** command is as follows:

val [[-m{name}] [-r{SID}] [-y{type}] [-s] {file . . .}] |−

For the **val** command, the argument {**file . . .**} can specify a single file, multiple files, or a directory. When multiple files or a directory is specified, the **val** command is limited to processing no more than 50 files at one time. For the **val** command, the minus sign (−) serves a special function, which will be described below.

As we shall see, the return code is the most important feature of the **val** command. Normally, a return code returns a single numeric value if an error is found. However, the return code for the **val** command is a composite code in which each of the 8 bits has a specific meaning, as defined in Table 9.1.

The **val** command begins with a return code for which all the bits are set to zero. For each test that fails, the appropriate bit is set. If either bit 0 or 1 is set, then the command line is in error and processing cannot continue for that command line. If either bit 2 or 3 is set, then there is a file problem and processing cannot continue for that file. If all the tests to this point have been passed, then the remaining tests are performed based on the options that have been set.

To understand how the **val** command works, let's look at a few examples. Starting with only a single file, the command

$ val s.exampl.c

validates the command line and then checks to see that the SCCS file was valid and that it was not corrupted. If either of these tests fail, a diagnostic message is printed on standard output and the appropriate bits in the return code are set. Since no options were given, no other test is performed.

If multiple files or a directory is specified, then, in place of a return code for

TABLE 9.1   RETURN CODE FOR VAL COMMAND

Bit	Value	Description
0	128	The argument {**file . . .**} was missing.
1	64	The option is invalid or a duplicate.
2	32	The SCCS file is corrupted.
3	16	The file does not have the read permission set or it is not an SCCS file.
4	8	If the **-r{SID}** option was given, then the SID is either invalid or ambiguous.
5	4	If the **-r{SID}** option was given, the SID is valid but does not exist.
6	2	If the **-y** option was given, the module type in the SCCS file does not match the {**type**}.
7	1	If the **-m** option was given, the module name in the SCCS file does not match the {**name**}.

Note: The bits are numbered from left to right.

each file, the return code is a composite of all the files that were tested. For example, the command

```
$ val *.c
```

might find both corrupted SCCS files and non-SCCS files.

The **val** command can also test the SCCS file for a match against any one of three variables: a specific SID (**-r{SID}**), the module name (**-m{name}**), and the module type (**- y{type}**). Of the three, only the SID is validated before a search of the SCCS file is performed. If the SID is ambiguous (only the **R** or the **R.L.B** is given) or is invalid (each element must be numeric and be greater than or equal to 1 and less than or equal to 9999), it is rejected and bit 4 is turned on. Each variable is independently compared to the SCCS file, so it is possible for more than one test to fail and, therefore, for more than one bit to be turned on.

The only other option for the **val** command is the **-s** option, which suppresses the printing of any diagnostic messages. These diagnostic messages correspond to the bits set in the return code. And while they help decipher the return code, such output messages are not always desirable in a shell script.

Let's look at a few problems and their solutions. In the first problem, we want to verify that all the files in a given directory are valid SCCS files. The simple solution is to use the following command:

```
$ if val -s *
> then
>   echo "All files are valid SCCS Files"
> else
>   echo "There is a bad file in the directory"
> fi
```

There are two problems with this solution:

1. The **val** command will fail if there are more than 50 files in the directory.
2. The test does not distinguish between a return code indicating non-SCCS files or corrupted SCCS files. In the above example, it could be both.

To overcome these problems, the files could be tested individually, as shown in the following:

```
$ for I in *
> do
>   if val -s $I
>   then
>     echo "File: $I is valid"
>   else
>     echo "File: $I is bad"
>   fi
> done
```

For the next problem, the number of conditions could be expanded so that only SCCS files that have a release number of 3, a module name called "join", and a module type equal to "m" would pass the test. Except for the release number, the solution is easy. How can a check be made for a release number when by itself it is an ambiguous SID? Easy! If the release number 3 exists, then the SID 3.1 has to exist. Now we can execute the test as follows:

```
$ for I in *
> do
>    if val -r3.1 -mjoin -ym -s $I
>    then
>          echo "$I"
>    fi
> done
```

As can be seen, the **val** command is useful for checking the truth of a series of conditions. However, if different actions are to be taken depending on which test failed, the shell programming becomes a bit more difficult. If only one bit is set, it will be a simple matter of testing for each value. However, when multiple bits are set, the return code is the sum of each individual error. For example, if bits 5 and 6 are set, the value of the return code is 6. Also, it is possible to use the following command line to see the binary value of the return code:

```
$ echo "obase = 2; $?" | bc
```

Back at the beginning of this section, it was noted that the minus sign ($-$) has a special meaning when used in the **val** command. With other SCCS commands, it means that the file names are to be entered through standard input. For the **val** command, it means that all the options and file names are to be entered through standard input. After each condition is entered, it is executed and, if any errors are found, they are printed on the standard output. The return code issued by the **val** command will be the combined result of each condition tested. The following is an example:

```
$ val -
-r3.1 -mjoin s.exampl.c
-r3.2 s.main.c
^D
```

9.5 The "vc" Command

As we shall see in Chapter 10 (see Section 10.6.2), the use of branches in an SCCS file to manage different custom versions (meaning a similar but separate entity) of a product is not always the best approach. If branches are not to be used, then how can different renditions of the same source file be maintained? Prior to UNIX System V, this could only be handled through the macro facilities of a language (**cpp** for C) or through the use of **M4**. With UNIX System V, the **vc** command provides another alternative. However, the **vc** command may be dropped after UNIX System V, Release 4.

The name **vc** for **v**ersion **c**ontrol is somewhat of a misnomer. Part of the problem arises from the overworked word, "version." In one sense of the word, every delta represents a version of the source file. From another point of view, each branch may represent different "custom versions" of the source file. To keep confusion to a minimum, the word **rendition** will be used to refer to the latter concept of version. Thus, the **vc** command allows the maintenance of different renditions of a source file within the same version. In other words, different products can be produced from a single version of the source file.

9.5.1 Syntax for the "vc" Command

The syntax for the **vc** command is as follows:

<pre>
        vc [-a] [-t] [-c{char}] [-s]
        [{keyword = value} . . . {keyword = value}]
</pre>

The **vc** command is a true UNIX filter. It reads the standard input and writes to the standard output. Any error or warning messages are written to the standard error. As a filter, **vc** processes the input based on the control statements in the text and then writes the revised text. These **version control statements** substitute values for keywords and can even select or ignore text based on defined conditions. Thus, before discussing the **vc** command options, the format and function of the version control statements need to be understood.

9.5.2 Version Control Statements

A **version control statement** is defined as any line of text that begins with a colon,":", the **version control character** or, simply, **control character**. This line of text is used strictly for processing by the **vc** command and is not written to the standard output. If a line of text that begins with a ":" needs to be written to the standard output, the colon needs to be escaped with a backslash: "\:". The backslash, however, will be stripped before writing the text line. The **vc** command will not automatically strip all backslashes from the beginning of a line. If a backslash is followed by any character other than the version control character, it will be passed to the standard output.

Note: Although the version control character can be changed to any other ASCII character, for the sake of simplicity, this discussion will consider the colon to be the symbol that represents the control character.

A **keyword** can be any string of not more than nine alphanumeric characters that begin with an alphabetic character. The **value** to a **keyword** can be any ASCII string that does not contain blanks or tabs. However, if a ":" or a "\" is included in the value, it must be preceded by the escape character "\". A **numeric value** must be an unsigned integer.

For a **keyword** to be replaced by a **value**, it must be surrounded by the **version control character**. For example, **ky001** could be a keyword. If it is written as **:ky001:**, it will be replaced by the associated value as long as it is part of a version control statement, or the **-a** option is given on the **vc** command line.

Before a keyword can be used in a source file, it must be declared as a keyword by the **:dcl** statement. The format of this statement is as follows:

:dcl {keyword}[, . . ., {keyword}]

There can be more than one **:dcl** statement in a source file and they may occur any place in the file. However, a keyword can only be declared one time.

A keyword can be assigned a value either by a command line argument (see below) or by the assign statement. This statement has the following format:

:asg {keyword} = {value}

When the **:asg** statement is used to assign a value, it will override any assignment made by a command line argument. Also, it is possible to assign different values to a keyword throughout the source file. Note that the assignment of a value to a keyword does not automatically mean that the keyword will be replaced by that value. However, if a value is not assigned to a keyword, a warning message to that effect will be printed on the standard error.

One use of keywords is as a means to substitute different values into a text line. Since substitution is not automatic, it can be accomplished by one of three means, as described in the following:

1. Any line of text that starts with two colons "::" is considered a version control statement. The double colon is stripped and keyword substitutions are made before printing the line on the standard output. The following is a short source file that will illustrate how text line substitution works:

    ```
    :dcl ky001
    :asg ky001 = example
    ::This is an :ky001: of how vc works.
    ```

    If this source file is processed by the **vc** command, the following will be printed on the standard output:

    This is an example of how vc works.

2. An entire block of text can be enabled for keyword substitution by bracketing

it with **:on** to start keyword substitution and **:off** to turn off substitution. The above example could also have been written as follows:

```
:dcl ky001
:asg ky001 = example
:on
This is an :ky001: of how vc works.
:off
```

3. The **-a** option can be given on the command line (see the next section for details).

Changing words in the text is only part of the solution to maintaining multiple renditions. With the **:if** statement, the **vc** command has the ability to include or exclude blocks of text based on a conditional statement. The format of the **:if** statement is as follows:

:if [not] {condition}
.
.
.
:end

If the {**condition**} is true, the bracketed text is passed to the standard output. The **:if** and **:end** are not sent to the standard output whether the test is true or false. The optional "**not**" is used to invert the sense of the entire condition. The most basic form of the {**condition**} is an {**expression**} which is defined as follows:

{**value**} {**operand**} {**value**}

The {**value**} argument can be a ASCII string (which contains no spaces or tabs), an unsigned numeric integer, or a keyword. If a keyword is used, it must be assigned a value or the **:if** statement will fail. The operands are as shown in Table 9.2. The following are some examples of valid expressions:

```
:ky001: > 12
:mach: != xyz
```

TABLE 9.2 "vc" OPERANDS

Operand	Description
=	Equal
!=	Not equal
<	Less than
>	Greater than

Expressions can be logically connected with the logical operators "**&**" (and) or "**|**" (or). The syntax for these operators is as follows:

{**expression**} **&** {**expression**}
{**expression**} **|** {**expression**}

The previous examples for an expression could be logically connected as follows:

:ky001: > 12 & :mach: != xyz

or

:ky001: > 12 | :mach: != xyz

To increase clarity and to control the order of comparison, parentheses, "( )", can be used to logically group expressions. The following are examples of how parentheses can be used in an **:if** statement.

```
:if ( :ky001: > 12 ) & ( :mach: != xyz )
text that is dependent on the condition
:end
```

```
:if (( :ky1: > 12 ) & ( :mch: != xy )) | ( :tst: = y )
text that is dependent on the condition
:end
```

Note that keywords must be separated from parentheses or logical operators by at least one space or tab.

In addition to the controlling of the text written to the standard output, it is possible to send messages to the standard error. An informative message can be sent with the following version control statement:

:msg {message text}

An example of the use of an informative message is

```
:if :mach: = xyx
:msg Machine xyx has been selected
Text to be sent to standard output
:end
```

For example, if processing is to be terminated when an invalid keyword is found, the error message format could be used. This type of message has the following format:

:err {message text}

The error message control statement will print the following on the standard error and halt processing with an exit code of 1:

ERROR: {message text}
ERROR: err statement on line 7 (vc15)

As mentioned in the beginning of this section, the default version control character is a colon. It is possible to change the control character within the source file by the use of the following statement:

:ctl {char}

That covers all the possible version control statements. Table 9.3 provides a summary of these statements, and Figure 9.1 shows an example of how they could be used in a source file.

9.5.3 "vc" Command Arguments

Since keywords play such a critical role in the processing of a source file by the **vc** command, the keyword argument is the most commonly used. Obviously, without the presence of this argument, there would be no purpose in using version control. The format of the keyword argument is

{keyword-1 = value-1} ... {keyword-n = value-n}

where syntax rules for keywords and values are as stated in the previous section.

TABLE 9.3   VERSION CONTROL STATEMENT
SYNTAX

:dcl {keyword} [, ..., {keyword}]
:asg {keyword} = {value}
:if [not] {condition}
{text lines} | {control statements}
:end
::{text line}
:on
{text lines}
:off
:ctl {char}
:msg {message text}
:err {message text}

```
:dcl mach, cust, ky001
:asg ky001=standard
:if not ( :mach: = xyz ) | ( :mach: = new )
:err mach value of :mach: invalid
:end
:if not :cust: = abc | :cust: = def
:err cust value of :cust: invalid
:end
:if :mach: = xyz & :cust: = abc
:asg ky001=custom
:end
:msg File for :mach: and :cust: is a :ky001: version
# %W%
::# %Z% For\: :mach: Project\: :cust:
This is an example of how version control works.
:on
Text for :mach: and :cust: will be substituted.
:off
Text for :mach: and :cust: will not be substituted.
:if :ky001: = custom
This is a custom product.
:ctl @
:This line will print without escaping the :
@ctl :
:end
:if :ky001: != custom
::This is a :ky001: product.
:end
End of test.
```

Figure 9.1 Example of Version Control Statements.

If Figure 9.1 were the source file to be processed, then the keywords could be assigned values by the following command:

$ **get -p -s s.exampl.t │ vc mach = xyz cust = abc > exampl.t**

9.5.4 "vc" Command Options

The **-a** option will force keywords that are enclosed in version control characters to be substituted in the entire text file. Thus, in Figure 9.1, the keywords in the line

Text for :mach: and :cust: will not be substituted

will be replaced with the assigned value. As can be seen, this option overrides any version control statements.

The **-t** option changes the rule that the control character must be the first character of the line. With this option, a control statement is defined as beginning with a tab, followed by a control character. This is true even if the tab is not the first character on the line. Any text preceding the control sequence will not be printed to the standard output. For example, if the **-t** option is present, the following lines are valid control statements:

> declaration<tab>:dcl ky001
> assignment <tab>:asg ky001 = test
> <tab>::Print :ky001:

The **-c{char}** option will change the control character. This will have a major impact on the processing of the source file. For example, the command

$ vc -c$ mach = xyz cust = abc < figure9–1

will turn off all version control processing since no statement begins with the new control character.

Recommendation! Unless there is a reason to do otherwise, do not use the **-c** option. If a different control character is needed, use the **:ctl** control statement.

The **vc** command will issue a warning message for such conditions as an unassigned keyword or a keyword that is declared but not used; the **-s** option will suppress these warning messages, plus any informative messages resulting from the **:msg** control statement. However, it will not suppress the printing of any error messages.

CHAPTER 10

Building the SCCS Source Tree

10.1 Introduction

In the last seven chapters, the SCCS file and the tools to create, maintain, and use an individual SCCS file have been discussed. A product, however, is composed of more than one source file. In this chapter and the next, we shall learn how to implement and use SCCS to manage the various source files that make up a complete product. In this chapter, we concentrate on the building of the SCCS source tree (see below for definition) for a product. Every issue, from SCCS file security to the loading of the source files into SCCS files, will be discussed. If the procedures as outlined in this chapter are followed for an actual product, you will have the SCCS source tree defined, loaded, and ready to use.

10.2 The SCCS Source Tree Structure

One of the most powerful features of UNIX is its hierarchical file structure. This feature can be a major aid in the organization of the source files for a product into a meaningful structure—a structure that will facilitate making changes to source files. For the moment, let's say that we have a clear understanding of which source files constitute the product. The problem then becomes which guidelines should be followed to create a logical and useful structure for the source files.

In manufacturing terms, a product is built from one or more components.

This concept applies to software or documentation, as well as to hardware. For example, the components of a 'C' compiler would consist of cpp, cc, opt, as, ld, libc.a, and so on; the components of a general ledger might consist of a chart of accounts maintenance module, a journal transaction entry module, a journal posting module, a trial balance module, and so on. The component concept is illustrated in Figure 10.1. To implement this concept for source files, we shall create directories for products and their components as shown in Figure 10.2.

Just as products consist of one or more components, components consist of one or more source files and, occasionally, subcomponents. For example, Component A in Figure 10.1 may consist of three source files, as shown in Figure 10.2.

Components (whether they are programs, libraries, or the chapters of a book) that consist of more than one source file are easy to define. But what do we do if a component consists of only a single source file? We could adhere to the rule that every component is a separate directory regardless of the number of source files in the component. Or we could group these single file components into a **component group** and place them in a single directory. Either choice is valid as long as the resulting structure presents a clear picture of the product.

What do we do when more than one component shares one or more source files? If the source files are shared by all components, then each of these common files can be maintained as a separate component. If the common files are shared by only a few components, then it would be better to create component groups consisting of the components and the common files. If this sounds a bit confusing, let's look at Figure 10.2 to see how it works.

We see that Product-1 consists of four components. Components D and E form a component group because they share a common source file not shared by

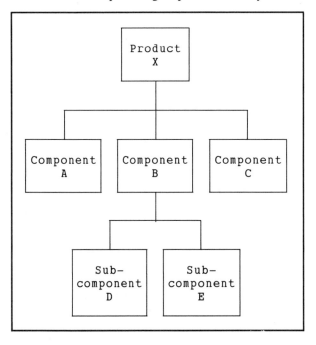

Figure 10.1 Product File Structure

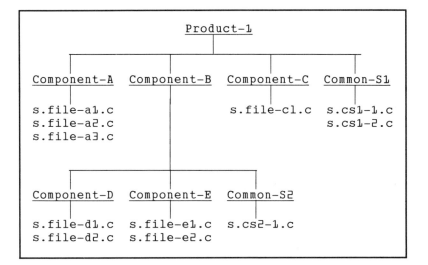

Figure 10.2   Example Product Source Tree

components A and C. Furthermore, we know that there are two source files that are shared by all the components. Just by looking at the source tree, it is possible to gauge the range of impact caused by modifying any source file. In addition, the source tree also indicates which source files are required to build a component.

What happens when several products share common files? For example, general ledger, accounts payable, and accounts receivable are separate products. Yet they share certain common programs and routines. In this situation, it is best to group the products into a group called a **product class**. At the top level, the source tree structure is as shown in Figure 10.3. Again, the structure helps to identify how the source files are related within the product class.

What can be seen from Figure 10.3 is that the common source files are, in fact, part of the tools used to build each accounting product. Thus, these common source files need to be treated as a separate product within the product class. By using this approach, we maintain explicit control over which version of the common source files is used to build each product. Such control will more than prove its worth when different teams are responsible for different products within the product class.

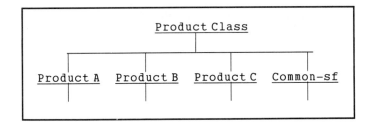

Figure 10.3   Product Class Structure

However, if the only bond between the products is the common source files, then it would be better to define the common source files as a separate product. This new product then becomes part of the tools used to build other products.

10.3 The Product Version File

As stated previously, SCCS does an excellent job at managing a single SCCS file or a small group of SCCS files. However, it starts to have problems when managing a complex source tree structure such as shown in Figure 10.2 or, even worse, Figure 10.3. The real problem occurs when you want to retrieve the source files that are necessary to build a specific version of a product. The first, and more than likely the last, time you will have the SIDs for all the source files match is when they are first installed under SCCS. Future versions of the product, however, will have SIDs of the component source files that are widely different, depending on the revision history of any one source file. Thus, how can you know which version of any one source file went into building a specific version of the product? As this information is not provided within the definition of standard SCCS, we need to enhance SCCS a bit by creating a special file to solve this problem, the **product version file**.

Now some of you are going to say that you do not need the product version file because you fix and install new versions of components but not new versions of the entire product. This may be true. But, unless every component consists of a single source file, the same question remains. Based on the information provided in the SCCS file, can you tell which version of each source file went into building a particular component? Same problem—right?

As to the composition of the product version file, it will consist of one line for each source file. That line will contain the component name (name of the parent directory), the SCCS file name, and the SID for this version of the product. The data items will be separated from each other by a single space or tab character. The product version file must also be an SCCS file so that a historical record is maintained on how to build any version of the product. Along with other files for defining and building the product, the product version file will be kept in **prod** directory for the product and will be called {*prod*}.*pv*, where {*prod*} is the name of the product.

For example, if the product directory is named **gl**, then the full path name for the product version file will be /srclib/gl/prod/s.gl.pv. The revised product source tree then looks like Figure 10.4, and the contents of the product version file are as shown in Figure 10.5.

10.4 Securing the SCCS Source Tree

For the remainder of this book, we are going to work on the basis of having a fully secured SCCS source tree. Achieving this level of security is going to require strict control of permissions and ownership of SCCS files and directories. It will also

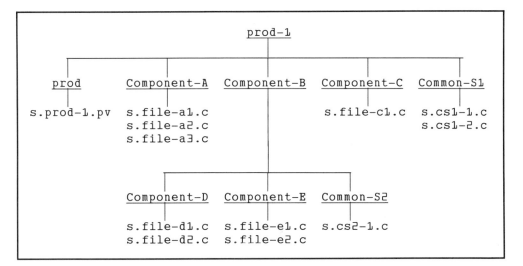

Figure 10.4 Revised Product Source Tree

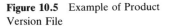
```
Common-S1 s.cs1-1.c 1.1
Common-S1 s.cs1-2.c 1.1
Common-S2 s.cs2-1.c 1.1
Component-A s.file-a1.c 1.1
Component-A s.file-a2.c 1.1
Component-A s.file-a3.c 1.1
Component-C s.file-c1.c 1.1
Component-D s.file-d1.c 1.1
Component-D s.file-d2.c 1.1
Component-E s.file-e1.c 1.1
Component-E s.file-e2.c 1.1
```

Figure 10.5 Example of Product Version File

require special versions of some SCCS commands, which will be discussed in Chapter 11. Once you understand how to implement a fully secured system, implementing a less secure system should be an easy task. By no means should the following be considered a comprehensive discussion of UNIX system security. For such a discussion, see references 1–3.

SCCS file security (which also includes directory ownership and permission) can be divided into three areas of concern: who can read files, who can create files, and who has permission to make deltas. Each of these topics is discussed in turn.

10.4.1 SCCS File Read Permission

Who has read permission is extremely important because, as we shall see, it represents the weakest link in the security chain. In comparison to those who have write permission, those who have read permission may represent the largest group of users. At a minimum, the individuals who create and change SCCS files must have read permission. Normally, there is also a larger group (such as customer support personnel) who must have permission to read SCCS files, but not to create or change them. Yet, for both files and directories, UNIX provides only three levels for controlling read permission: owner, group, and others. With only these three levels of permission, how can we control read permission?

Before deciding on how to assign read permission, we need to consider the following issues:

1. *Certain source files are highly sensitive and only a limited group should have access to them.* For instance, a company's software protection mechanism would be of little value if it were common knowledge. Just as important, documentation regarding specific projects may also be highly sensitive and should have restricted access.

2. *Software licensed from another party may impose restrictions on the number of individuals who are allowed to have access.*

3. *Permission to read is permission to copy.* Once a copy of a source file is in an individual's account, there is little that can be done to protect against further distribution of that source file.

4. *Permission to read is also permission to change.* The only problem is that the changes may be unofficial. Consider what would happen if a person could read the source to a payroll program, could make a few changes, and then were able to install this new version in place of the official version. Or a customer needs a quick change. The person who makes the change is not on the development team, but really wants to help the customer. He retrieves the necessary source files, makes the change the customer wants, and then forgets to tell anybody about the change. The next official version is released and the customer's change is lost.

For most SCCS files, the above points mean that **read permission to "others" is forbidden**! Giving read permission to "others" is the same as giving read permission to everyone that has access to the computer. Not only should "others" be denied read permission to the file, but they should be denied read permission to the directory. After all, to a trained eye, a listing of the contents of a directory can reveal a lot of indirect information about a product. To be consistent, if you deny read permission to the directory, then you must also deny search permission. Obviously, if you are not allowed to see the contents of a directory, why should you be able to use it as part of a path name?

At the opposite end of the scale, we do not want to limit read permission to only the owner of the SCCS file. This leaves the group permission as the only means to explicitly define those who, besides the owner, have read permission. For SCCS files, this means that the file mode must be 440, not the 444 to which SCCS defaults. Since the directory permission depends on other factors, suggested permissions will be discussed in the next section.

10.4.2 Creation of SCCS Files

The ability to add and delete SCCS files in the SCCS source tree is a permission that should be granted to a limited number of people. Under UNIX, this ability is controlled by the write permission of the directory. Without question, write permission should never be granted to "others." For if it was granted, everyone would have the ability to create files in the SCCS directory. Furthermore, since group permission is used to define read access, the group will probably contain individuals that will not have update permission. Thus, the group must not have write permission. This leaves only the owner with write permission. Unless there is good reason for a more liberal approach, the directory permission for each directory in the source tree should, therefore, be set to 750.

10.4.3 SCCS File Delta Permission

The final issue to be resolved is defining who can make deltas to SCCS files. In this situation, SCCS comes to the rescue by providing the user table section of the SCCS file. How to initialize and modify this table was discussed in Chapters 4 and 7, respectively. One very important detail: the individuals defined in the user table must also be members of the group that is assigned to the file and to the directory. Otherwise, it will be extremely difficult to modify an SCCS file that you cannot read.

There is, however, a fly in the ointment. The group does not have write permission in the directory. This will cause any SCCS command that needs to create a work file (**p-file**, **x-file**, and so on) in the SCCS directory to fail. Getting out of this predicament is the cause for most people surrendering on maintaining strict SCCS file security. It is far simpler to give the group write permission or to give access to the owner account to everyone who needs to make a delta. But these are neither the best nor the only answers.

The problem is how to get write permission for those persons that need to make changes to SCCS files without giving them all the privileges of the owner. The solution is to create a program that interfaces to the SCCS commands (see Appendix E for more details on this program, including source). This program will be owned by the owner of the SCCS files (another reason for each product to have a separate owner) and will have the mode bit turned on for "set user ID on execution" (SUID). When executed, the SCCS command invoked will inherit the privileges of the owner. One of the main advantages with this approach is that it is possible to limit which SCCS commands can be invoked. For example, only **get -e**, **delta**, **unget**, **rmdel**, and **cdc** could be executed by those users defined in the user table. Use of the commands such as **admin** (which would allow a person to change the user table) and **comb** could be denied to all except the owner of the SCCS files.

Note that the lack of write permission does not prevent the use of commands (**get**, **prs**, **sact**, **sccsdiff**, **val**, **vc**) that do not create work files in the SCCS file directory. But what about the **g-file** created by the **get** command? The answer is that the **g-file** is created in the current working directory, which, as we shall see in Chapter 11, should never be in the SCCS source tree.

10.5 Hints on Building the SCCS Source Tree

Given the above guidelines for SCCS source trees and security, you are ready to set up an SCCS source tree. Before going on to the next subject, here are a few additional hints:

1. Unless there are overriding reasons, all SCCS files for all products should exist under one directory. As a suggestion, the directory should be named /srclib for source library. /srclib should be owned by root and have a mode of 755.
2. Within the /srclib directory will be a separate directory for every product and product class.
3. To control access to each product or product class, they must have a different owner. By having separate owners for each product, we can separate the management of the SCCS files for a product among different individuals without giving every person access to every product.
4. The product directory is to be owned by the owner of the source files for the product and have a mode of 750. A product class directory may have to have a mode of 755 if each product has a different owner.
5. To have tight control over who has read permission to a file, only the owner of the SCCS files should have the read permission group defined as the default group in the /etc/passwd file. All others can use the **newgrp** command to change their group ID. This makes control of read permission a mere matter of adding or deleting names from the list of valid user IDs for a group (see Figure 4.3).
6. If an existing product is being placed under source file management, its current tree structure may not be compatible with the above guidelines. Serious consideration should be given to modifying the structure at this point. You may never have another chance to organize the chaos that has existed for years.
7. Establish the structure for a product before creating the SCCS files. Once the structure is defined, you will know where to put the source files.

By the way, one more component group should be a part of every product: documentation. The directory could be called **doc** and would contain all product-related documentation (for example, specifications, system documentation, and user documentation).

10.6 Defining SCCS File Parameters

The last task before starting to initialize the SCCS files is to make decisions about the SCCS file parameters. For convenience, the following discussion is ordered by SCCS file segment. Remember that, except for the ID keyword (**i**) flag with an ID keyword verification string, the parameters can be changed (see Chapter 7) at any time.

One disadvantage, and advantage, of SCCS is that, with the exception of the **m**, **q**, and **t** flags (see below for explanation), the parameters are the same for all the SCCS files in a product. In exceptional cases, the user table might vary so that different individuals have delta privileges for different components. This means that the same information has to be entered in every SCCS file, which makes implementation and changes both more work and more prone to error. On the other hand, for the special cases, this redundancy is to SCCS's advantage in terms of increased flexibility. The last section in this chapter will look at ways to make this task easier without losing flexibility.

10.6.1 Defining the User Table

The need for defining users that have delta permission was discussed above and does not need to be repeated. What needs to be discussed at this point is how to define the user table. As discussed in Chapter 4, the entry of either individual user IDs or group IDs is permitted by the **admin** command.

While using group IDs simplifies the initial entry and maintenance of the user table, they are not compatible with the above security scheme. Given that the group ID is used to control read permission, if the group ID in the user table is the same as the group ID of the directory, it is the same as having no entry in the user table. If it is a different group ID, then access to the SCCS files is a problem. As mentioned above, to maintain a secure system, the directory permission must be 750. This means that, except for the owner, the search path for the SCCS files is defined by the group ID. Therefore, it is not possible to define a group consisting of only those with write permission, since this group would not have directory search permission.

Since the use of group IDs is out, this leaves defining individual user IDs as the only choice. The only decision at this point is whether to grant access or deny access (see Chapter 4) to members of the read permission group. The choice depends on which alternative will create the smallest number of entries. If most of the group will have delta permission, deny access to those who do not, and vice versa.

10.6.2 Defining the Flag Table

When building the SCCS source tree, we are only concerned with the flags defined in Chapter 4. So that you can easily cross reference this section with Section 4.6, the order of presentation will be the same. Note that the delta access flags section can be skipped (see Section 4.6.1).

Delta creation flags. Before discussing the question of whether or not to use branches as a means of managing different renditions of a source file, it should be clear that **there is no way to totally prevent branches from being created in an SCCS file**. As previously mentioned in Chapter 4, the branch flag only determines whether or not a direct descendant of a delta must exist before a branch can be created. Given the above, the question is whether or not the creation of branches should be used as an active means to manage different renditions.

If there is only one rendition of the product, then the decision about branching is easy: don't. There is no need to create confusion in a straightforward situation. However, if one of the following conditions exists, then branching has to be considered:

1. There are custom variations of a product for different customers. This is a common situation for computer dealers that provide custom modifications of an accounting package for different customers. It can also be the case in a system software house that provides different variations of a compiler to different companies.

2. Multiple products are derived from the same source files. In a sense, this is similar to the above. However, the emphasis here is on the manufacturing of products for different environments. For example, a compiler could be produced to run under different CPUs.

The decision would be easy if it were not for the existence of alternative ways to manage different renditions of a product. Instead of using branching, the different renditions can be maintained through the macro preprocessor facilities of some languages (for example, cpp for 'C') or through use of **vc** (see Chapter 9). The question then is when is it better to use a preprocessor versus branching.

Perhaps the following points will help make the decision a little easier:

1. Must the different renditions be kept in sync? A company sells a 'C' compiler for different CPUs. When a new version is released for a product, it should be released for all CPUs at one time. In this case, use the macro preprocessor facilities provided. If branching were used, then changes to the common code would have to be incorporated into every branch. On the other hand, with macros the change automatically affects every rendition. Conversely, if the changes in the main product should not constantly force new releases of the variant products, use branching. Through the include facility of the **get** command, it is always possible to bring the branch forward. This is not a trivial task, but it is far better than trying to manually make the changes.

2. How many renditions does the product have? If there are a lot of renditions of a product, then it may be better to use branching. Macros can get very messy and complicated to sort out when there are too many of them.

By the way, it is possible that both are required. Back to the 'C' compiler example. Let's say that several customers have different custom variations of the compiler. Furthermore, each variation is capable of producing a product on several

CPUs. Customers only get the latest version when they have specifically agreed to having their variation upgraded. In this scenario, macros would be used for the different CPUs and branching for the different customers.

If branches are to be used as a means of managing the product, then the next question is whether or not to allow branches to be created from a leaf delta. Normally, branches should be allowed from a leaf delta if branching is part of the product management strategy. So, unless there is a specific reason otherwise, the answer to this question is to set the branch flag.

The other flag in this group is the **n** (null delta) flag. If you have decided not to support branching, then you need not be concerned about setting the **n** flag. As described in Chapter 4, the null delta flag is used to create null deltas for skipped releases, the concept being that these null deltas can become anchor points for new branches. Thus, in theory, it should create more consistent release numbers. The problem is that theory and practice sometimes do not meet. Before making the decision of whether or not you want to set the **n** flag, consider the situation in Figure 10.6.

Let's say that a new branch needs to be created from release 2 instead of from the current release. In this situation, null deltas would have only helped for s.file-a3.c. The flag was not necessary for s.file-a1.c and s.file-a4.c. For s.file-a2.c, the setting of the null delta flag was of no help as the file has not been accessed for some time. For this file, a null delta would have to be manually created to change the release number.

What happens if a new branch had to be created from the current release and all the release numbers kept the same? In this example, the null delta flag provides no assistance, since a release has to be skipped for a null delta to be created. This means that every file that was not changed would require a null delta to be manually generated.

As you can see, the **n** flag only helps if branches are created from past releases and all the source files are at the same release level. Also, since a null delta is another entry in the delta table, it adds to the size of the SCCS file. Given the limitations and price paid, the **n** flag is of minimal value and should not be used.

Get command parameter flags.   In this group, the only flag of interest at the time of initializing the SCCS file is the joint edit (**j**) flag. Again, if you are not supporting branching, then setting this flag is not necessary (see Chapter 4 for an explanation). If the branch flag is set, then the joint edit flag should be set if more

File	SIDs: () represents null data created as a result of the n flag
s.file-a1.c	1.1 1.2 1.3 2.1 2.2 3.1 3.2
s.file-a2.c	1.1 1.2
s.file-a3.c	1.1 1.2 1.3 (2.1) 3.1
s.file-a4.c	1.1 1.2 2.1 2.2

Figure 10.6   Example SIDs for **n** Flag

than one branch is being created at one time from the same delta, or if a branch delta is being created at the same time as a new trunk delta is being created. The last case is a little dangerous in that the branch will not derive benefit from the latest changes to the trunk. This needs to be considered more carefully.

Picture this scenario. Ted is fixing a major problem in file-a3.c and is in the process of creating delta 3.2. Joe is working on a custom version for a special customer and needs to create a new branch. If the joint edit flag has been set, he will create a branch with the delta 3.1.1.1, thereby ignoring the work of Ted. The customer experiences the problem and threatens legal action. Joe says he used the latest version and Ted said he fixed the problem. Both are right. But with the joint edit flag set, Joe was allowed to edit the same SID as Ted.

However, if several custom renditions have to be created at the same time, the joint edit flag has to be set for this to happen. This flag is a two-edged sword; set it with a full understanding of the potential dangers.

Keyword definition flags.   Since the **q** flag has no meaning assigned to it by SCCS, we recommend that it be used to define the product to which the source file belongs. If the naming system described above were followed, the variable would be assigned the name of the product directory. Following these conventions will facilitate the identification of the module when incorporated as part of the SCCS ID string (see below for suggested SCCS ID string format).

Again, as part of the identification process, the **m** flag should be used to identify the component or subcomponent to which the source file belongs. In terms of the above naming convention, this would be the name of the parent directory for the SCCS file. As with the **q** flag, the **m** flag should be incorporated into the SCCS ID string.

While the **q** and **m** flags are used to identify the module, the **t** flag can be used to group the SCCS files and, if included in the SCCS ID string, the source files. For example, if this were the source tree for 'C' programs, the module type flag might distinguish between include files, functions, main modules, and so on. SCCS does not have any predefined groups, so the choice is yours. It is suggested that short codes be used, as the more characters that have to be entered the higher the probability of having multiple variations of the same code.

As we shall see, the SCCS ID string performs a very critical function in the identification of modules in the final product. To ensure that every source file has an ID string, the **i** flag should be set. In fact, the question should not be why should the **i** flag be set, but, rather, why should it not be set. If an ID keyword verification is also to be provided, keep it simple (see Chapter 7 for a complete discussion of this issue).

Delta command parameter flag.   What SCCS calls Modification Requests may be called by many other different names (for example, Software Problem Report, Software Discrepancy Report, Trouble Report, and Bug Report). Normally, for purposes of document management, a number is assigned to these documents. In SCCS, it is called a **modification request number**. If the problem tracking system has been automated, then it is possible, by using the **MR number**, to link completion of a request with the corresponding delta. For customer support, this can be an invaluable tool, since, when combined with the **what** command, it is possible to see if the customer has the correct module. Without the link, it is very difficult to provide this kind of information.

Appendix D shows a simple shell script that will examine an ASCII file containing valid MR numbers and, if it finds a match, will create an entry in the log file. If it does not find a match, an error is returned. While this is an extremely simple routine that needs a lot more to make it part of a viable tracking system, it does show how the interface mechanism works.

10.6.3 Defining the Descriptive Text

Just as source files and deltas may have comments, SCCS files may have comments in the form of descriptive text. If branches have been created, it is a great place to keep information about the branch. The SID tells us something about a branch's heritage, but it tells nothing about why it was created. A simple comment in the descriptive text section can solve this problem. Just as a reminder, the descriptive text can be initialized with the following lines:

```
R.L.B<tab>date<tab>Description
-------<tab>-------<tab>-----------------------------
```

Also, when a branch history report is required, the descriptive text can be printed with the **prs** command (see Chapter 8).

The descriptive text section might also be used to document changes in release numbers. A heading similar to the above could be added to the SCCS file when it is initialized.

10.7 ID String Standards

The need for an ID string (also called a "**what**" string because of the link to the **what** command) has been previously discussed (see Chapter 8). The question now is what should be the format of this string or group of strings. At a minimum, an ID keyword string, such as the following, should be included in every source file:

```
%W% %F% %Y% %D% %Q%
```

This string will expand (see Appendix B) to the following:

```
@(#)<module><tab><SID> <File name> <type> <date> <prod>
```

The above format is suggested for the following reasons:

1. If the SCCS source tree concept as defined above is used, then this string format can uniquely identify a source file within the tree structure. Given the product, component, file name, and SID, the exact delta could be retrieved.

2. The date can be a useful indicator of when the module was retrieved for building. Normally, this would be a close approximation of the actual date the product was built.

3. The module type can be used to identify the nature of the source file.

4. By using %W% as the leading ID keyword, it is possible, if necessary, to use the **-w** option of the **get** command to modify the string.

Figure 10.7 shows how to include the above ID keyword string in different types of source files. The one problem with this string is that, unless the SCCS file is in the current working directory (which should never be the case), the %F% will expand to the full path name of the SCCS file. This seems to be the result of a bug in the **get** command, which fails to strip the path name from the file name.

While the above ID keyword string can be used to identify a source file, it tells us very little about the product or the component. From the above string, the only clue as to the version of the product is the retrieval date. This need not be the case. Since ID strings are not limited to ID keywords, they can be used to provide a full description of the product. The following is a model of a more descriptive set of ID strings:

```
{product name}
version: {product version} Release Date: {Date}
{company name}
{copyright statement}

{component name}
{source file ID keyword string}
   .
   .
   .
```

While this model is oriented toward a product that is distributed outside the company, it is possible to develop a similar format for internal company products. The trick is how to implement this concept. For 'C' programs, the product and component information can be made part of the main module via the include statement. However, this assumes that the main module is the first module in the executable program. Another approach is to make the product and component ID strings a separate 'C' module that is compiled and linked to be the first module in an executable program. Figure 10.8 shows an example of how a 'C' routine could be written. The **vc** command (see Chapter 9) could also be used to supply the variable information about the product and component. For example, the identification module for the "spell" component of version 1.2 of the "Ideal Word Processor" could be created with the following commands:

```
$ get -p -s s.idhdr.c | vc prodver=1.2 reldate=2/23/89 \
> cname=spell > idhdr.c
$ cc -c idhdr.c
```

```
'C' programs:
    char id[] = "%W% %F% %Y% %D% %Q%";
Shell scripts:
    # %W% %F% %Y% %D% %Q%
Make files:
    # %W% F% %Y% %D% %Q%
FORTRAN programs:
    character*80 id
    data id/'%W% %F% %Y% %D% %Q%'/
Pascal programs:
    var id:array[1..80] of char;
    begin
            id:='%W% %F% %Y% %D% %Q%';
    end.
COBOL programs:
    77 ID             PIC X(80) VALUE "%W% %F% %Y% %D% %Q%".
```

Figure 10.7   ID Strings in Various Types of Source Files

```
/* Example of Product Header String */
/* %W% */

:dcl prodver, reldate, cname
char id1[] = "%Z%Ideal Word Processor";
::char id2[] = "%Z%version\: :prodver:  Date\: :reldate:";
char id3[] = "%Z%Ideal Software Company";
char id4[] = "%Z%Copyright data";
char id5[] = "%Z%\\n";
::char id6[] = "%Z%Module\: :cname:";
```

Figure 10.8   Example of 'C' Identification Module

The latter approach can also be used for putting ID strings into libraries. All that has to be done is to archive the identification module as the first module in the library. In some cases, such as the 'C' libraries, it may not be a good idea to have an ID keyword string in every module in the library. For libraries, the question has to be asked as to whether the additional strings will clarify or confuse the reader of the "what" strings.

For shell scripts, the information must be part of every shell script or be tacked on by the **cat** command when the product is built.

The source for the identification module can be kept in the common directory for the product (see Figure 10.9 for an example). As can be seen, these files are maintained as SCCS files just as any other source file for the product.

```
                        /srclib/sfm
         ┌─────────┬──────────┼──────────┬──────────┐
       prod       doc      scripts      sfint       common
    s.sfm.pv    s.sfm.man  s.getst.sh   s.sfint.c   s.sfmhdr.c
    s.makefile  s.makefile s.sget.sh    s.makefile  s.sfmhdr.sh
                           s.sdelta.sh
                           s.dted.sh
                           s.deltast.sh
                           s.verst.sh
                           s.sfinit.sh
                           s.pvinit.sh
                           s.mrval.sh
                           s.setsfm.sh
                           s.makefile
```

Figure 10.9   SCCS Source Tree for "sfm"

10.8 Loading the Source Files

All the decisions having been made, all that is left is to create and, depending on circumstances, to load the initial deltas into the SCCS files. The following is the suggested order of events for loading the source files:

1. Put the source files into the proper directories. Or, if this is a new project, model source files could be created that include the necessary ID strings. These models could then be copied to the appropriate file names. For example, assume that there are two source files called model.c and model.sh (shell model). A copy of these models could be used as the initial source for defining each source file in the SCCS source tree.

2. If the source files contain no ID strings, add the required ID strings to the source files.

3. When creating the SCCS file, add the first delta. The SID of the initial delta should be related to the current release level of the product.

4. Remove the source files, since the **admin** command does not automatically remove source files, as does the **delta** command.

5. Build the product version file.

Shell scripts can be written to make some of this work a little easier. Appendix F includes a shell script called **sfinit** that will perform steps 3 and 4. Similarly, Appendix F also defines a shell script (**pvinit**) that will build the initial version of the product version file. Appendix F includes a complete description of each shell script, examples of how to use it, and the source for the shell script.

> Note that, rather than adding more programs to /usr/bin, it is better to create a new directory called /usr/sfm for all the source file management programs.

As an exercise in implementing SCCS, define and create an SCCS source tree for the tools described in the appendixes to this book. As a suggestion, the product can be called "**sfm**" for source file management. Thus, the SCCS path for the product would be /srclib/sfm. Figure 10.9 shows one possible SCCS source tree structure. Again, this is only a suggested approach; you may wish to define an altogether different approach. The above only defines the building of an SCCS source tree. How to actually build the product or products is beyond the scope of this book.

If the suggestions in this chapter have been followed, the source tree is now loaded and ready to use, which is the subject of Chapter 11.

References

1. Patrick H. Wood and Stephen G. Kochan, *UNIX System Security* (Hasbrouck Heights, N.J.: Hayden Book Company, Inc., 1985).
2. X/Open Company Ltd., *X/Open Security Guide* (Englewood Cliffs, N.J.: Prentice Hall, 1989).
3. Rebecca Thomas and Rik Farrow, *UNIX Administration Guide for System V* (Englewood Cliffs, N.J.: Prentice Hall, 1989).

CHAPTER 11

Using
the Source Tree

11.1 Introduction

SCCS is well designed to handle source file management for a single file, but it needs a little help when it comes to managing the source files for an entire product. Providing this help will be the topic of this chapter. Several approaches will be used to accomplish this objective, including other UNIX utilities and some new programs. By the end of the chapter, a working source file management system should be in place, a system that is both easy to use and, at the same time, fulfills all the requirements set forth in Chapter 1.

11.2 Structure of the Work Source Tree

As can be seen from the directory permissions defined in Chapter 10, the SCCS source tree for a product does not facilitate using the directory as a work directory. In fact, the SCCS directories must, with the exception of emergency repairs, never be used as the working directories. Instead, the SCCS source tree for each product forms a **Source Library** from which we make withdrawals and returns.

The source tree structure in which we make all our changes will be called the **work source tree**. The structure of the work source tree for a product will be identical to the structure of the SCCS source tree for that product. All the directory names will be the same; all the file names will be the same. The only difference will be that the SCCS source tree will consist of SCCS files and the work source tree will consist of the corresponding source files for a particular version of the product. For example, the work source tree for the SCCS source tree shown in Figure 10.4 would be as shown in Figure 11.1.

Why must the structure of the work source tree match that of the SCCS source tree? The following are two of the reasons:

1. It makes life a lot easier to retrieve and delta a group of files if the two tree structures are identical. The SCCS structure tells how a group of files is to be retrieved, and the work structure provides the information on the location of SCCS files for the source files to be deltaed. Using Figure 10.9 as an example, the SCCS source tree path would be /srclib/sfm. A corresponding work source tree path might be /usr/joe/sfm. The pvinit.sh is part of the "scripts" component. Thus, the relative path would be ./scripts. The path to the SCCS file would be /srclib/sfm/scripts, and the path to the work file would be /usr/joe/sfm/scripts.

2. Whether all or only a part of the structure is being modified, all the makefiles (instruction files used by the make command) or other tools used in building a product will have a constant frame of reference, the relative path discussed above.

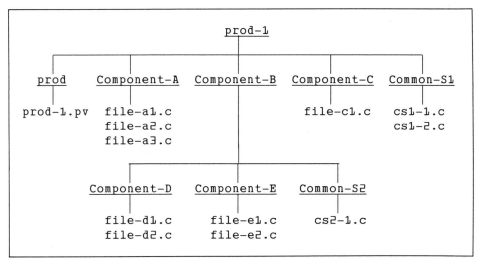

Figure 11.1 Example Work Source Tree

11.3 Retrieving the Work Source Tree

Each time you need to retrieve the entire work source tree for a particular version of a product, the following tasks must be performed:

1. The work tree structure needs to be created. This tree structure will replicate the tree structure of the SCCS source tree.

2. A work file that defines the path to the SCCS source tree, the work source tree, and the version of the product on which work is being performed needs to be created.

3. The product version file for the specified version of the product must be retrieved. As discussed in Chapter 10, the product version file defines the required SID for each source file that makes up a product.

4. Based on the information in the product version file, retrieve the specified version of each source file into the correct component directory.

If only one component is needed, the process is the same as defined above. The only difference is that, instead of building the entire tree structure, only the tree structure needed for the components in question needs to be created. Since the product version file is the reference to what needs to be retrieved, the **prod** directory must always be created.

A new command is needed to perform the tasks of creating the tree structure and retrieving the correct source files. The command is **getst** and is described in Appendix F. Since the **getst** command only retrieves a particular version of a product, it can be used by anyone who has group read permission.

11.4 Editing the Work Source Tree

Once the work source tree structure has been created and the source files retrieved, we are ready to modify the source files that need to be changed. As discussed in Chapter 10, retrieving a source file for edit creates a special problem in that the group does not have write permission in the directory. A special interface program (see Appendix E) that has SUID permission (set user ID) is needed to solve this problem. When this program is executed, the effective UID will become the same as the UID of the owner of the program. The interface program will then "exec" the specified SCCS command and pass its environment (including the effective UID) to the SCCS command. If the owner of the interface program is the same as the owner of the SCCS file, it is as if the file were being accessed by the owner of the file.

Programs with SUID permission are potentially dangerous security loopholes. To limit access to this program, the mode for this program should be 4710, where the 4 is used to make the program SUID. With these permissions, anyone in the group can become SUID to the owner. What limits delta permission is the list of UIDs defined in the SCCS file.

Warning! The use of a group ID in the user table changes the rules and can make the system very difficult to use. See Chapter 10 for a full discussion.

While the special interface program allows us to retrieve a file for editing, it does not automatically support the product version file concept presented in Chapter 10. To support this concept, a special version of the **get** command needs to be created. This new command must fulfill the following requirements:

1. If a source file is being retrieved for edit, the SID for the product version file will be checked to ensure that it is the latest version (that is, a leaf delta). This check is very important. Depending on the length of time between the retrieval of the source tree and the first retrieval for edit, it is possible for someone else to have updated the product, thus making the information in the product version file out of date. If an out-of-date product version file is used, it will be equivalent to creating a new rendition of the product.

2. The default SID to be retrieved for edit will be the one specified by the source file in the product version file. A warning message will be printed on standard error if the retrieved SID is not a leaf delta. This indicates that the product version file is no longer in sync with the source tree.

3. The special interface program is used to retrieve the source file.

4. In addition to retrieving the required source files for editing, the product version file is also retrieved for edit. This means that only one user at a time can retrieve a product for editing. When a development team is involved, this means that all the members of the team must share the same work source tree. The pros and cons of this approach will be discussed in Chapter 12.

5. While the bug documented in the manual pages for get(l) seems to have been fixed, a **get -e** for multiple files needs to be broken up into a series of **gets** for single files. This bug has been noted in the documentation since UNIX Version 7 days. However, somewhere along the line, it seems to have been fixed. This is one of the problems with the "bugs" section of the manual pages. We do not know whether it is current fact or ancient history. So, to be on the safe side, the possibility that it still may be true needs to be covered.

The above requirements are fulfilled by the **sget** command, which is described as part of the local commands in Appendix F.

11.5 Updating the SCCS Source Tree

For the same reasons that we need an **sget** command, we need a corresponding **sdelta** command. This command is fully described in Appendix F. However, let's take a look at how everything ties together.

To be able to keep the product version file current with the version of each source file that composes the product, the product version file is retrieved for edit the first time an **sget** command is executed with the **-e** option. When an **sdelta** command is executed, in addition to deltaing the source file, it updates the SID in the product version file for that source file. This keeps the product version file in sync with each SCCS File in the product.

The normal consequence of deltaing a file is that it is deleted from the work source tree. Using the **-n** option of the **delta** prevents the file from being deleted. However, the ID keywords remain in the unexpanded format. To expand the ID keywords, the **-n** option of the **sdelta** command executes a **get** command for the SID it just deltaed. Thus, we are always ready to build a product with the correct ID keywords.

The one danger with this approach is that there is no automatic deltaing of the product version file. How to deal with this problem will be discussed below.

11.6 Maintenance of the SCCS Source Tree

With the exception of a few special issues, maintenance of the SCCS source tree is no different than maintenance of a single SCCS file. For the purposes of maintaining file integrity and for reasons of security, it is important that only the owner of the SCCS file be able to use the **admin** command. The one exception is the updating of the descriptive text section of the SCCS file, which is discussed below. Before tackling that issue, we must look at the problems caused by changing the structure of an SCCS source tree.

11.6.1 Making Changes to the SCCS Source Tree

The creation the tree structure and retrieval of source files for the work source tree is based on the structure of the SCCS source tree and the information in the product version file. As long as the structure of the SCCS source tree does not change, there will be no problem with the retrieval of any version of a product. However, if a source file name is changed, or a component name is changed, or a source file is moved to another component, or a component is broken into subcomponents, then the linkage between the product version file and the SCCS source tree is broken. Let's look at ways to handle some of these changes.

1. Adding a new component with a new source file(s) creates no problems. The **getst** command builds the structure based on the component names defined on the command line or the component names defined in the product version file. Components that are not defined are not created.

2. Whether changing the name of a SCCS file or moving it to another component, the solution is the same. A new SCCS file has to be created with the minimum structure necessary to support the trunk and any branches. For example, if the file had no branches and the last SID was 4.7, we could use the following command line to change the name:

    $ get -k -p s.oldname | admin -n -i -r4 s.newname

Of course, the user table, flag table, and descriptive text would have to be updated in the new SCCS file to match those of the old SCCS file. If branching were involved, the solution is not so simple, since the minimal structure necessary to support the different branches needs to be maintained. In this case, the following example offers one solution to the problem:

```
$ cp s.oldname s.newname
$ comb -o s.newname
```

In either case, the old SCCS file would have to locked to prevent any further changes from being made to it. To do this, the following command would be executed:

```
$ admin -fla s.oldname
```

Finally, an entry would have to be made in the descriptive text of both the old and the new file to indicate the action taken. How to make this entry will be discussed in the next section.

3. A change in the component name can only be resolved by keeping both the old and new component names. The SCCS files would be transferred from the old to the new component as described above.

4. The solution to splitting components into subcomponents is best accomplished by keeping the old component name for historical purposes and creating a new name for the new component structure. Then the remainder of the solution is the same as above.

While the above solutions may not be elegant, they will preserve the ability to retrieve any version of the product ever created.

11.6.2 Updating the Descriptive Text

As mentioned previously, the descriptive text section of the SCCS file is used for commentary about the SCCS file. The problem is that maintenance of this section must be done by the **admin** command. From the point of view of file security and integrity, the use of this command must be limited to the owner of the SCCS file. The solution to the need to update the descriptive text section and still preserve security is to create the **dted** (**d**escriptive **t**ext **ed**it) command, which performs the following functions:

1. The current descriptive text, if present, is retrieved into a temporary work file.

2. The work file can be edited by any editor, as defined by the environmental variable EDITOR or as specified on the command line.

3. The updated work file will then replace the existing descriptive text.

Before performing the above operations, the **dted** command checks the user table to verify that the user executing the command has delta permission. As with the other local commands, this command is fully described in Appendix F.

11.7 Resolving Some Remaining Problems

While the above solves the major problems regarding the maintenance of a product, it does leave a few loose ends that need to be resolved. This section discusses those problems and looks at possible solutions.

11.7.1 Maintaining Environmental Variables

One of the more tedious aspects of the regular SCCS commands is that we have to constantly type the SCCS path name to the desired file. To alleviate this tedious task, the special commands described in this chapter take advantage of the data stored in the .sfmdata file. As part of each shell program, the environment is established via the **setsfm** shell script (see Appendix F).

The special interface program will also use these variables if they are part of the environment when the program is executed. To set the variables in the environment, simply execute the following command:

$. setsfm

The leading dot is very important. Without this dot, the environment for **setsfm** would never be exported back to the parent shell.

Not every SCCS command is covered by the above cases (for example, **prs**). Although specific examples are not given in this work, there should be no problem creating a shell script based on the concepts presented here.

11.7.2 Deltaing the Product Version File

While the product version file may be automatically retrieved for edit, it must be manually deltaed. Since it is updated automatically as each delta is made for the source files in a product, it is easy to forget about its existence. To help make this task a little easier, Appendix F describes the command **deltast** (delta source tree). The **deltast** command searches the work source tree to verify that no other files are still retrieved for edit before it deltas the product version file—a simple command, but one that helps overcome the problem of failing to delta a source file and makes sure that the product version file is deltaed.

11.7.3 Keeping Track of Branches

Branches create a very messy tracking problem that presents no easy solution. As was shown in Figure 10.6, it is normal to have source files with widely varying SIDs. Using Figure 10.6 as an example, if we were to create a new branch from the current version of each source file, the SIDs generated would be 3.2.1.1, 1.2.1.1, 3.1.1.1, and 2.2.1.1. Nothing in this group of SIDs tells us that they are all part of the same version of a product. The problem then is how to link these varying SIDs into a single product.

Short of making sure that every source file in a product has the same delta tree, the only way to deal with this problem is to document what is happening. The best place for this documentation is in the descriptive text section of each SCCS file. In Chapter 10, the initialization of the descriptive text section with column header lines was discussed. Using the **dted** command, described earlier additional entries can be made to each source file when a branch is created for that source file.

Ultimately, all the source files that compose the new branch to the product will be tied together in the product version file. Since the automatic retrieval for edit of the product version file by the **sget** command always gets the latest version on that branch (either **mR.mL** or **R.L.B.mS**), this means that it is necessary to retrieve the product version file for editing before retrieving any other source file. Only by doing this can a new branch for the product version file be created. Just like any other SCCS file, the descriptive text section needs to be updated to describe the new branch.

There is one hidden danger to this approach. In a majority of cases, the new branch for a product contains a mixture of new branches for some source files and many source files that are still part of the trunk. Thus, as development of the main product continues, the SIDs for SCCS files that are part of the trunk will get further and further out of date. To resolve this problem, we have to look at the larger problem of keeping the product version file in sync with the SCCS source tree.

11.7.4 Keeping the Product Version File in Sync

If there are no branches, if every source file is always updated using the commands described above, and if the product version file is always deltaed, the product version file will always be in sync with each SCCS file. However, such is not the case. By definition, branches will start to get out of sync with the trunk for any given product. And even procedures that are followed with the best of intentions will sometimes suffer minor catastrophes. The simple solution is the command **verst** (see Appendix F), which verifies that every SID in the product version file is a leaf delta. If it is not, a warning message is issued and, if the **-u** option is given, the product version file is corrected.

CHAPTER 12

A Look
at the Management
Side

12.1 Introduction

The previous chapters have looked at source file management from the technical perspective. This chapter will take this knowledge and show how it applies in actual practice. The problem of the SCCS source tree and the work source tree existing on different machines will also be addressed. Since conversion of nonversion controlled source files is of major interest, we shall cover some suggested steps for converting these source files to SCCS. And, last but not least, some issues about the human dimension of source file management will be reviewed.

Few issues have more potential to create turmoil within an organization than the implementation of a source file management system. Yet the initial storm is only the beginning of the ongoing task of source file management. The one basic law about source file management is that the tendency toward chaos is **always** present. This tendency can be kept in check only by having both a well thought out source file management system and a strong organizational commitment to maintaining that system. The goal of this chapter is to link all the pieces together so that a successful source file management system can be implemented and maintained.

12.2 The Source Library Concept

Not too many years ago, the source library was the filing cabinet for decks of punched cards and paper tapes. Today, the file cabinets are full of magnetic tapes and floppy disks. In many organizations, the only difference between today and the old days is that the media has changed. While on-line source library systems have been around for some time, they have often become just another storage medium for the filing cabinet approach.

The primary concept behind the filing cabinet approach was that source file management could only be achieved by erecting barriers between the source files and developers. Under this system, the developer had to come to the "source file librarian" (sometimes called quality control or configuration management) and get a copy of the source files. Of course, before the request could be filled, the proper form had to be completed and signed by the appropriate managers. Depending on the efficiency of the source file librarian, the request could be filled immediately or in a few days. Occasionally, when there was a change of librarians, source files managed to get lost in the filing system.

The developer's response to the filing cabinet approach was to go around the system. They did this by keeping their own "working" copy of the source files. This working copy was the copy to which the developer made all of his or her changes. When a product was ready to be released, the working copy was submitted to configuration management as the "official" copy for that version. Initially, the source file librarian accepted that this was a valid official copy and just filed the media in the appropriate filing cabinet. Then, one day, somebody actually tried to build a product based on the source files given to the source file librarian and couldn't do it. It seems that the developer had either forgotten to include a few source files, used different versions of the tools, used tools not mentioned in the build instructions, never really built the product as one single unit, or some combination of the above.

To solve this problem, management made a few changes to the order of events. Development would now build a "development" version of the product that was to be used only for development testing. They then required that the "official" version of the product be built from the "official" version of the source files and that this be done by a group (often called configuration management) that was not connected to development. Thus, configuration management operated as the police for ensuring compliance to source file management policy. In a sense, configuration management became active source file librarians, which under the filing cabinet philosophy was a passive role. However, for the same reasons as before, it always took several rounds for the official version of the source files to build the correct product. Each error correction round took time, and time meant delays in schedules, and delays in schedules generated a sharp response from management to get back on schedule. The development group blamed configuration management for their unreasonable policies, and configuration management blamed the development group for their failure to correctly do their job.

We would expect that after one correct "official" version had been built, the problem would go away or at least be significantly reduced. On the contrary, since the development group felt that getting the official version was too difficult, its working version was used to build the next generation. Inevitably, all the errors that were corrected in making the official version work never got back to the working version, and the whole cycle was repeated again. Could this cycle ever be broken?

To eliminate the filing cabinet mentality, a different approach is needed. This change can be provided by a source library that is composed of an SCCS source tree for each product, as described in Chapter 10. This source library is then made available on a real-time basis to all parties requiring access. Thus, the development team can check out a product to make changes, delta the changes back into the SCCS source tree, and pass configuration management the SID of the product version file, which defines the version of the product to be built. Configuration management can then check out the SCCS source tree and build the product. While the actual methods for building a product are beyond the scope of this book, it is important to understand that all the necessary information can be made available through the source library. The difference between the above and the filing cabinet approach is that a readily available official copy of the source tree is modified by the developers. And the identical source tree that was used by development to build the product is readily available to configuration management.

Given this concept, let's look at what it takes to make it work.

12.2.1 The Source Library Machine

While there may be exceptions, as a general rule the source library should exist on a single computer under one standard directory such as /srclib. If the same computer is used as both the source library and the development computer, then the concepts discussed in Chapters 10 and 11 and the special commands described in the appendixes are all that is needed to establish an effective source file management system.

However, in today's world of desktop computers, the source library may be maintained on a machine that is separate from the development computer. In this environment, we shall call the machine on which the source library resides the **source library** machine and the machine on which development is performed the **development machine**. For the purposes of this discussion, the term development machine refers to any computer that may contain a work source tree. Thus, the development machine includes configuration management and customer support, as well as the development group. The problem then becomes how to provide the development machine access to the source library machine.

12.2.2 Access to the Source Library Machine

It makes no difference whether the development machine and source library machine are separated by 10 feet or 1,000 miles, because the SCCS commands and the special commands described in the appendixes require direct access to the

SCCS source tree. This means that they have to be executed on the machine in which the source library resides. For this reason, these commands will be referred to as **local** commands. Direct access to the SCCS files can also be achieved through UNIX System V's remote file sharing (RFS) or network file sharing (NFS) facilities. How to implement an RFS or NFS network is beyond the scope of this book. For our purposes, it is enough to understand that through RFS or NFS it is possible to access the source library machine as if it were part of the development machine's file system. The same result can be achieved for those operating under a local area network (LAN) that supports a distributed file system (DFS).

What happens when it is not possible to implement an RFS, NFS, or DFS environment? After all, once the source library machine becomes separate from the development machine, it opens the door for possibilities such as the following:

1. Computers using other versions of UNIX could use the source library machine.
2. The source library machine could become the repository for all source files, regardless of the operating system used by the development machine. For example, if an accounting package was developed for both DOS and UNIX, the source could exist on one machine. Furthermore, it would be possible to use a macro preprocessor, such as the **vc** command, to manage the two renditions.

To implement source file management on a remote development machine (remote meaning not part of an RFS, NFS, or DFS network), a set of **remote** commands is needed that will communicate with the local commands on the source library machine. Since the actual design will vary depending on the operating system of the development machine and the mode of communication between the development machine and the source library machine, only the general concept of the remote commands will be discussed in this work.

Eliminating those commands that are only used for the initialization of the SCCS source tree, the required remote commands and the corresponding local commands are shown in Table 12.1. Let's look at some of the implications in building a source file management system around the use of remote commands.

TABLE 12.1 LIST OF REMOTE COMMANDS

Local Command	Remote Command
getst	rgetst
sget	rget
sunget	runget
sdelta	rdelta
dted	rdted
deltast	rdeltast
verst	rverst

For the remote commands to work, the following environment must be established:

1. Each owner of an SCCS file must have an account on the source library machine.
2. Each user who needs access to the source library must have an account on the source library machine.
3. Preferably, all user accounts operate in a restricted shell that limits the available commands to those necessary to execute the remote commands. The objective is to prevent the user account on the source library machine from being used for purposes of development.
4. For each command, all source files will be removed as soon as the necessary action has been completed. For example, the work source tree created on the source library machine by the **getst** command will be removed as soon as a successful file transfer has occurred.

A typical scenario might look like the following:

1. The command **rgetst** is executed to build the work source tree and retrieve the source files. Since all the requisite parameters have been predefined, it is as if the source library was on the remote development machine. The only difference is the time it takes to transfer the source files over the communications link between the source library machine and the remote development machine.
2. The command **rget** is executed to retrieve for edit the files that need to be changed. To reduce communications time, the file is retrieved with and without expansion of the ID keyword strings. The difference between the two is taken, and the delta file transferred to the remote development machine. The source file on the remote development machine is then modified to look like it would have had it been transferred in its entirety.
3. When development is completed, the sources files that have been changed are deltaed with the **rdelta** command. The files are transferred from the remote development machine back to the source library machine. The **sdelta** command is then executed to actually make the delta.
4. Once all changes have been completed, the **rdeltast** command is executed to verify that all changes have been deltaed and then to delta the product version file.
5. The SID of the product version file is given to configuration management. They, in turn, can retrieve the identical source tree and build the official version of the product.

Given that it would be next to impossible to ever get a developer to give up his or her copy of the work source tree, the **rgetst** command should be designed to verify the tree structure against the official SCCS source tree. Only those source files that are different need to be transferred. Furthermore, the **rgetst** command must also make sure that the structure of the work source tree is the same as the SCCS source tree. As mentioned previously, keeping the structure the same is important in ensuring that what can be built once can be built a second time on a different machine.

12.3 Controlling Product Changes

For a single product, it is possible for a number of work source trees to be in existence at the same time. Every user who has permission to read the SCCS source tree could have a work source tree. Yet, as defined in Chapter 11, only one person can be making changes to any one branch of the product at any one time. Why is this limit placed at the product level, instead of at the component or even the source file level? To answer this question, we need to look at the consequences of having different source files for the same product being updated by different users at the same time.

As long as two people do not try to edit the same source file at the same time, the retrieval of various source files for edit by different users does not create a problem. All that is implied at this time is an intent to make a delta. The information necessary to create that delta is recorded in the **p-file**. So, by design, it is impossible for two people to edit the same source file for the same release of the product. Thereby, the integrity of the individual source file is always maintained. But what about the integrity of the component or the product?

As previously stated, the purpose of the product version file is to track the SIDs of each source file that make up the product. For the product version file to reflect the current status of the product, the **sdelta** command must update the SID in the product version file when a delta of a source file is made, thereby providing the means to achieve component and product integrity. As can be seen, the difference between source file integrity and product or component integrity is that the latter is maintained when the source file is deltaed. The problem then centers around the mechanics of updating the product version file.

Should the **get -e** drive the retrieval of the product version file or should the making of a delta? It is given that, once the product version file has been retrieved for edit, no one else can make a delta to this rendition of the product until the product version file has been deltaed. Thus, if **get -e** controls the product version file, then only one work source tree can be used for editing of the product at a time. If the delta drives the updating of the product version file, then multiple people can be working on separate work source trees of the product at one time. To see if the limit of only changing one work source tree makes sense, let's look at the consequences of multiple users making independent changes to the product.

In order not to lock out deltas for any length of time, the product version file would have to be retrieved, changed, and deltaed every time an **sdelta** command is executed. This would mean that, instead of one, or at least a very small number of deltas for any one release of the product, the number of deltas to the product version file would equal the number of deltas made to every source file. At best, this approach represents a tremendous waste of disk space. At worst, it is possible to intermingle changes to different releases of the product. Thus, there is no clear demarcation between the end of one product development cycle and the beginning of the next.

Even worse than the lack of demarcation is that, if we were trying to build a new version of the product and several people had been changing the product, no one would have the correct set of source files for the entire product. Programmer A's work source tree would represent the state of the product at the time that the work source tree was built, plus any changes that he or she has made. But what about all the other changes? What about the interaction between changes? For example, if one source file that is common to the entire product was changed, this could affect other changes. If those changes where being made to another copy of the work source tree, then their impact would be masked. To build and test the product, a new work source tree would have to be retrieved that would reflect the most current delta of the product version file.

All the above confusion can be avoided when there is only one work source tree that is used for making changes to a product. If a special change has to be made and it must be kept separate from the rest of the changes, create a new branch. The changes made as part of the new branch can be reintegrated into the main development effort with the include option of the **get** command.

12.4 A Look at the Organization Chart

Will the implementation of a source file management system have an impact on the organization chart? To some degree it will. This is one of the consequences of implementing the concepts presented in this book.

For example, Yourdon's chief programmer team concept[1] includes a person who is the librarian. The librarian is the team's "go-for" and, as such, served a function in the days when compiles had to be submitted to the computer room for execution and when source file management meant keeping track of decks of cards. However, in today's development environment, the function of a librarian is no longer necessary. In a similar sense, the role of the configuration management group as the source librarians has also changed. Then what kind of organization is needed to support the concepts presented in this work? The following sections attempt to answer this question.

12.4.1 The SCCS Administrator

The SCCS administrator is responsible for the source library and, if it is on a separate machine, the source library machine. In this capacity, the system administrator's duties include the following:

1. Primary responsibility for source file security. Only the SCCS administrator should be able to update the /etc/passwd and /etc/group file entries that are required to protect source file access.

2. Development and maintenance of all the source file management tools (for example, those defined in the appendixes of this book).

3. The establishment of new product directories and the creation of the related tools.

4. In terms of the actual product, the SCCS administrator can only act to ensure compliance with standards. The actual initialization and maintenance of the SCCS source tree is the responsibility of the owner of the product.

The SCCS administrator could be a separate function or it could be a part of the configuration management group. It makes little difference where it is placed in the organizational chart. However, to avoid undue influence, the SCCS Administrator should never be a part of the development group.

12.4.2 The Development Team

The chief programmer, the team leader, or whatever other title is attached to the person who has primary responsibility for a product should also have access to the source library as owner of the product. As such, this person will have primary responsibility for defining and maintaining the structure of the product. Only the owner of the SCCS files will have the ability to define new components, create new SCCS files, or change the user table or flag table in existing SCCS files.

However, for retrieving a work source tree, a development account that is not the same as the account for the owner needs to be used. Otherwise, anyone who has access to the owner account has the ability to make any change to the SCCS source tree that the owner can make. Just remember, only one copy of the product can be retrieved for edit. It becomes the responsibility of the development team to manage access to that copy.

12.4.3 Configuration Management

The impact on the configuration management group, or its equivalent, is probably greater than on any other group. No longer is it acting as file clerks for keeping track of the products submitted. Instead, the function of moving a product from the development stage to the production stage becomes its primary task.

Given that the development team no longer has to wait for copies of source files and that a common source tree is being used to build products, the tension between configuration management and development should be lowered. If nothing else, this should help reduce or eliminate the discrepancies between the official version of a product and the development version of the product.

12.5 Resistance to Source File Management

With rare exception, giving up control of their source files is very traumatic for developers. It is their security blanket. For as long as they have the source files, they feel that the organization needs them. As long as transferring media back and forth between the source librarian and the developer is the primary means of source file management, it is easy for the developer to use delay in getting a copy as the reason for never relinquishing control. By changing the role of configuration management, by limiting the role of the SCCS administrator, and by keeping control of the product within the domain of the development team, the resistance to source file management will be greatly diminished.

Ultimately, for the resistance to source file management to be reduced, it is going to take total commitment on the part of management to make it part of the development process. Always keep in mind the axiom that it is managers who, by and large, want source file management. Developers would prefer to have no control outside of what exists within the development team.

12.6 Conversion of Existing Software

Establishing order where chaos reigns can only be accomplished when there is a strong commitment to turn the tide. This means that the resources necessary to undertake this task have to be made available even if this means that other projects may have to be temporarily delayed. This is not easy, because the single major cause for source file management getting a low priority is the pressure caused by the demand for change combined with the lack of resources to implement those changes. At best, it is very difficult to convince customers, whether they are internal or external to the company, that a delay for initiation of a source file management system is more important than the next release of the product. At worst, management will just have to absorb the flak and proceed with the conversion. To do this will take a commitment that goes through all levels, all the way to the top boss.

To make the task even more challenging, during the actual conversion and loading of a product, all work on that product will have to cease in order to establish a baseline. If a product is not frozen during the actual conversion, the official version will never match the working version. This is the one chance to get everyone in sync on one official version of product.

There is no denying that implementation of a source file management system is a major undertaking that will have to be tackled in phases. To keep the confusion of conversion to a minimum, there will have to be a conversion schedule for each product. Keeping to the schedule becomes extremely critical as the manager for each product will have to schedule the conversion in coordination with ongoing work on the product. If at all possible, a product should be converted at the time that one version has been completed and before work on the next version begins.

The following is a suggested series of steps for conversion.

1. Decide on standards for file security, ID strings, maintenance request numbers, and product naming conventions.
2. Decide on the location of the source library. If it is to be a separate machine, install the machine in a secure location and establish the communications links to other machines.

3. Develop, test, and implement any special source file management programs required. The programs given in the appendixes of this book may be sufficient or, at least, may provide a base for further development. These source files will automatically become the first product to be loaded into the source library.

4. Establish the baseline for a product. If the product is composed of several custom versions, a choice will have to be made as to whether to integrate the different versions into a single trunk or whether branches are needed (see Chapter 10 for guidelines on making this choice). If branching is chosen, then the baseline will have to be such as to provide the minimum delta structure for supporting all the branches. If the branches are not based on the current version of the main product, this means that some common ancestor will have to be chosen as the initial delta.

5. Make all necessary modifications to the software, such as changes to structure, adding ID keywords, and writing makefiles. This is not the time for fixing all of the nuisance problems that you never had time to fix. The objectives of this step are to organize the product into a structure that supports the concepts presented in Chapter 10, to make sure the product can be correctly built.

6. Verify that the work source tree created in step 4 will build the product. In theory, it should build an exact binary image of the product represented by the baseline that was chosen in step 3. However, adding or changing the ID keywords will cause false differences in the binary images.

7. Establish the SCCS source tree structure as a mirror image of the work source tree structure. Notice, at this point, that only the directories are being created. In the next step, all the source file will be added to this structure.

8. If the source library exists on a separate machine, transfer the work source tree to the source library machine.

9. Using the **sfinit** command, create and load the initial delta for all the required SCCS files, with appropriate entries for the user table, flag table, and descriptive text (see Chapter 10 and Appendix F). Since the SCCS file is being created in this step, the command must be executed by the owner of the SCCS file.

10. Once all the source files have been loaded into SCCS files, the product version file can be initialized using the **pvinit** command (see Appendix F). After checking to see that the product version file is OK, use the **sfinit** command to create the initial SCCS file for the product version file.

11. At this point the baseline for the SCCS source tree has been completed. As a check, the work source tree should be retrieved with the **getst** command to verify that the correct source tree is created. Any corrections can be made using the **sget** and **sdelta** commands. If branches are to be loaded, continue with the next step; otherwise, skip to step 20.

12. If branches are to be created, the SCCS source tree may not represent the current state of the product. Before installing any branches, the trunk needs to be brought forward to a version that will create the current product. For

a better understanding of what is required, look back at Figure 3.11. If we were trying to convert this to an SCCS file, version 1.3 would have to be the baseline in order to support the branches. Then version 2.2 would have to be loaded, since it represents the current version of the product.

13. To create a branch for a product, first retrieve the correct baseline for the branch with the **getst** command.

14. Using the **sget** command, create a branch of the product version file.

15. Retrieve the source files for which branches have to be created by using the **sget** command. Remember to specify the **-b** option.

16. If necessary, add ID keyword strings to all the new sources files.

17. Build the product just to be sure that a build can be performed under the current structure.

18. Using the **sdelta** and the **deltast** (see Appendix F), delta all the new branch deltas into the SCCS source tree.

19. Repeat steps 13 through 18 for each branch to be created.

20. Clean up all the directories that may have leftover items from the conversion. This is especially true if the source library machine has been used for the conversion.

21. Bring out the **champagne**. A major step has been accomplished and it deserves a celebration.

As stated previously, conversion is only the beginning. If active steps are not taken to make using the source library an integral part of the development and maintenance cycles for a product, all this effort will be lost.

12.7 A Review of the Requirements

Have the requirements for a source file management system that were defined in Chapter 1 been met by the system that has evolved in the intervening chapters? Let's take a look:

1. It is possible to retrieve any version of a product. All that needs to be done is to use the **getst** command with the appropriate SID.

2. All the source files used to build the product have been maintained. And, if procedures have been followed, the structure of the retrieved product is the same. Thus, if the same tools are available, then an exact replica can be made.

3. Again, if the methods outlined in this book are followed, we will always know the ancestry of every source file and of every product. It is all there in the SCCS files with records of dates, times, and comments about every event.

4. The security procedures outlined in Chapters 10 and 11 will ensure the security of the SCCS source tree. However, once the source has been checked out of SCCS, responsibility for security passes to the owner of the work source tree.

5. Only one user can retrieve a file for edit along any one branch, including the trunk. While it is possible to get around the protection provided by SCCS, it would not be possible to do so without full knowledge about what is being done.

6. The source library concept presented above makes access to any version of the source files for a product as simple as possible within the bounds of today's technology. When using a source library machine, the limit to speed of access is a function of the mode of communication.

7. Without using file compaction techniques, the delta concept used by the SCCS file minimizes the amount of space required to perform source file management.

8. If products have well-structured source trees, and if there are few problems with being able to replicate the building of a product, then the cost of implementing a source file system will be minimal. However, it is at the time of conversion to a source file management system that we also must pay for our past sins. The cost of conversion is directly proportional to the current amount of chaos. Once conversion has been completed, the system takes a minimal amount of effort to maintain. This does not mean zero effort. Lack of ongoing support will result in a return to chaos.

9. Given that there will always be some resistance to a source file management system, the system presented above should minimize the resistance. In time, use of the source library will become second nature. Yet this can only happen as long as management sees source file management as important.

There may be more elegant and more efficient ways to do source file management. However, as a part of standard UNIX, the ready availability of SCCS combined with the additional tools presented in this book make SCCS a logical choice for building a source file management system.

References

1. Edward Yourdon, *How to Manage Structured Programming* (New York: Yourdon, Inc., 1976), p. 127

SCCS Flag
Definitions

Flag	Description
	Delta access flags
f{floor}	The lowest **release** number that can be retrieved for editing by the **get** command. The number must be greater than 0 and less than 9999. If this record is not present, the default value is 1. The purpose of this flag is to lock historical releases from continuing to be the base for branches. For instance, if the floor was defined as 2, then deltas 1.1 to 1.n would be locked.
c{ceil}	The highest release number, or ceiling, that can be retrieved for editing by the **get** command. The number must be greater than 0 and less than 9999. For the ceiling, the value of 9999 means unspecified and is the default value. Note that the release number does not have to exist to be set as the ceiling.
l{list}	This flag locks the {list} of deltas so that the **get** command can no longer retrieve the specified deltas for editing. The syntax is
	{list} = {Release number}[, ...] | a
	where a means all deltas are to be locked. Just as a selected release can be locked by setting the flag, it can be selectively unlocked by deleting the release numbers defined by {list}.
	Delta creation flags
b	The creation of branches from a leaf delta is not allowed unless this flag is set.
n	Change of the release number is under the control of the **get** command. There is no rule that says that the release number must be consecutive. Thus, it is possible to have release 1 followed by release 4. This flag forces null deltas for the missing releases.
	Get command parameter flags
d{SID}	The delta name specified by **SID** becomes the default used by the **get** command.
j	Normally, the **get** command prevents more than one person from editing the same delta at the same time. When this flag is set, it is possible to retrieve multiple copies of the same delta for editing.
	Keyword definition flags
i[{IDkwd}]	Both the **get** and **delta** commands check for the presence of ID keywords (see Appendix B) in the source file. If no ID keywords are found, the message "No id keywords (ge6)" is printed. The default is to treat this as a warning message. If the **i** flag is set, then it is treated as a fatal error and the command will be aborted.

Flag	Description
	If an ID keyword string {IDkwd} is present, the string will be used as a validation string. The ID keyword string in the source file must be equal to the length of {IDkwd}.
m{mod}	If this flag is present, then the module name defined by the variable {**mod**} will be substituted in place of the %M% of the ID keyword and :M: of the **prs** command keywords. If the flag is not set, the default is to substitute the SCCS file name without the "s." for the above keywords.
q{text}	User-definable text that substitutes for the %Q% ID keyword or :Q: keyword of **prs**.
t{type}	The **type of module** is a user-defined value that can be used in the building of ID keyword strings or by the **prs** command.
	Delta command parameter flags
v[{pgm}]	The presence of this flag will make entry of modification request numbers mandatory. If a program name {pgm} is specified, it will be used to verify the MR number entered.

SCCS Identification
Keywords

Keyword	Description
%R%	Release number
%L%	Level number
%B%	Branch number
%S%	Sequence number
%I%	SCCS identification (SID) of the retrieved text
	%I% = %R%.%L%.%B%.%S%
%F%	SCCS file name with relative path
%P%	SCCS file name with full path
%M%	Module name, which is the SCCS file name with the leading "s." removed or, if set, the value of the **m** flag (see Appendix A)
%D%	Current date with the format YY/MM/DD
%H%	Current date with the format MM/DD/YY
%T%	Current time with the format HH:MM:SS
%E%	Date of the retrieved SID formatted as YY/MM/DD
%G%	Date of the retrieved SID formatted as MM/DD/YY
%U%	Time of the retrieved SID formatted as HH:MM:SS
	Note: The values for %E%, %G%, and %U% are from the delta table of the retrieved SID
%Q%	The value of the **q** flag in the SCCS file (see Appendix A)
%Y%	Module type: the value of the **t** flag in the SCCS file (see Appendix A)
%Z%	The special string characters **@(#)**, called the "what string," recognized by the **what** command,
%W%	A shorthand notation for the "what string," where %W% = %Z%%M%<horizontal tab>%I%
%A%	Another variation of the "what string," where %A% = %Z%%Y% %M% %I%%Z%
%C%	The current line number in the source file; this is for debugging purposes only and should never be used to number the lines in a file

SCCS Data
Keywords

Keyword	Description
	Delta table keywords
:DL:	Delta line statistics (the @s record) where :DL: = :Li:/:Ld:/:Lu:
:Li:	Count of lines inserted by the delta
:Ld:	Count of lines deleted by the delta
:Lu:	Count of lines unchanged by the delta
:Dt:	Delta information (the @d record) where :Dt: = :DT: :I: :D: :T: :P: :DS: :DP:
:DT:	Delta type where D = normal and R = removed
:I:	SCCS identification (SID) of the delta where :I: = :R:.:L:.:B:.:S:
:R:	Release number
:L:	Level number
:B:	Branch number
:S:	Sequence number
:D:	The date in which the delta was created where :D: = :Dy:/:Dm:/:Dd:
:Dy:	The year in which the delta was created
:Dm:	The month in which the delta was created
:Dd:	The day in which the delta was created
:T:	The time at which the delta was created where :T: = :Th:::Tm:::Ts:
:Th:	The hour in which the delta was created
:Tm:	The minute in which the delta was created
:Ts:	The second at which the delta was created
:P:	The login name of the user who made the delta
:DS:	Delta sequence number
:DP:	Predecessor delta sequence number
:DI:	Composite of the include, exclude, and ignore lines where :DI: = :Dn:/:Dx:/:Dg:
:Dn:	Deltas included in this delta (the @i record)
:Dx:	Deltas excluded from this delta (the @x record)
:Dg:	Deltas ignored in this delta (the @g record)
:MR:	List of MR numbers for delta *Note:* This text will take one line for each MR number entered for the delta.

Keyword	Description
:C:	Comment lines for delta
	Note: this text will take one line for each comment record present. The maximum length of the comment record is usually 512 characters.
	User table keywords
:UN:	Login names or group IDs authorized to make a delta. *Note:* This text may take multiple lines.
	Flag table keywords
:FL:	Composite list of entire flag table
	Note: This text will require one line for each flag that has been set. The format is different than that for individual flags. The format for each flag is as follows:

Flag	Format
f	floor\<tab\>:R:
c	ceiling\<tab\>:R:
l	locked releases :R:...
b	branch
n	null delta
d	default SID\<tab\>:I:
j	joint edit
i	id keywd err/warn
m	module\<tab\>{module name}
q	csect name\<tab\>{user text}
t	type\<tab\>{module type}
v	validate MRs\<tab\>[{validation pgm}]

Note: The flag table keyword names are different than the names for the flags (see Appendix A). For reference, the flag name is given in parentheses.

Keyword	Description
:FB:	Floor boundary (f); lowest release that can be retrieved for editing
:CB:	Ceiling boundary (c); highest release that can be retrieved for editing
:LK:	Locked releases (l)
:BF:	Branch flag (b); value will be "yes" or "no"
:ND:	Null delta flag (n); value will be as above
:Ds:	Default SID (d)
:J:	Joint edit flag (j); see :BF: for values
:KF:	ID keyword flag (i); see :BF: for values
:KV:	Keyword validation string
:M:	Alternate module name (m)
:Q:	User-defined keyword (q)
:Y:	Type of module (t)
:MF:	MR validation (v); value will be "yes" or "no"
:MP:	Name of MR validation program
	Descriptive text keywords
:FD:	Descriptive text for the SCCS file
	Note: This text may take multiple lines.
	Body of source keywords
:BD:	Complete listing of source including commands
	Note: This text may take multiple lines.

Keyword	Description
:GB:	Source for the specified delta *Note:* This text may take multiple lines.
	Other keywords
:W:	Same as %W% ID keyword (see Appendix B)
:A:	Same as %A% ID keyword (see Appendix B)
:Z:	Same as %Z% ID keyword (see Appendix B)
:F:	SCCS file name
:PN:	SCCS file path name

MR Validation
Program

Name

mrval   Validate MR numbers.

Syntax

mrval {source file} {MR number} ...

Description

mrval is a Bourne shell script that can be used with the **delta** command. If the validation flag is set in the SCCS file, the **delta** command passes the program name followed by the list of MR numbers to **mrval**. Each {MR number} is validated against a file of valid MR numbers. If all the MR numbers that were passed are valid, then a log record is written for each MR number in the following format:

delta {source file} {MR number} mm/dd/yy hh:mm:ss

Options

No options.

Example

$ mrval exampl.c mr001 mr002

See Also

The **srmdel** command, described in Appendix F, provides for a log entry to be created for deleted deltas.

Source

Note: The line numbers shown below are not part of the actual SCCS program. They are included in the source listing only for purposes of reference.

```
 1 :
 2 # %W% %F% %Y% %D% %Q%
 3
 4 # mrval - MR Validation Program
 5
 6 USAGE="usage: mrval {pgm name} {MR ...}"
 7
 8 # Exit Codes and their meanings
 9 # 0 - Normal
10 # 1 - Argument count wrong
11 # 5 - Invalid MR
12
13 ERET1=1
14 ERET2=5
15
16 # VFILE is the name of the file that contains the list of
17 #        valid MR numbers. The only requirement is that
18 #        the first field contain the MR number.
19 # LFILE is the log file of MRs that have been validated.
20 VFILE=/usr/mradm/valmr
21 LFILE=/usr/mradm/logmr
22
23 # test for required options
24
25 if test "$#"-lt 1
26 then
27    echo $USAGE 1>&2
28    exit $ERET1
29 fi
30
31 # process the arguments
32
33 SFILE=$1
34 shift
35 MRS="$*"
36 for I in $MRS
37 do
38    if (grep "^$I" $VFILE 1>/dev/null 2>&1)
39    then
40      true
41    else
42      exit $ERET5
43    fi
44 done
45 for I in $MRS
46 do
47    echo "delta $SFILE $I `date '+%D %T'`" >> $LFILE
48 done
```

Discussion

Since the **delta** command will fail if any MR number is not valid, the entire list must be validated before updating the log. If more than one source file is changed because of an MR, then the MR number will appear in the log for each source file that references that MR number.

SCCS Command
Interface Program

Name

sfint{xx}	SUID interface to SCCS commands.
get{xx}	SUID interface to the **get** command.
delta{xx}	SUID interface to the **delta** command.
unget{xx}	SUID interface to the **unget** command.
rmdel{xx}	SUID interface to the **rmdel** command.
cdc{xx}	SUID interface to the **cdc** command.

Note: The argument {**xx**} is to be replaced by the product code for each product. Thus, there could be a **sfintgl**, a **sfintcc**, and so on, one for each product.

Syntax

sfint{xx} [-C{SCCS Command}] [options] [arguments]
get{xx} [get options] {SCCS File Name}
delta{xx} [delta options] {SCCS File Name}
unget{xx} [unget options] {SCCS File Name}
rmdel{xx} [rmdel options] {SCCS File Name}
cdc{xx} [cdc options] {SCCS File Name}

Description

The purpose of the **sfint{xx}** command is to provide an SUID interface to the selected SCCS commands referenced above. As shown in the example below, the argument {**xx**} represents the name of the product and is used to distinguish the different versions of this command. While it is possible to define and use **get{xx}**, **delta{xx}**, and **rmdel{xx}**, it is not recommended. To ensure the integrity of the product version file, the **sget**, **sdelta**, and **srmdel** commands described in Appendix F should be used instead.

Each version will be owned by the owner of the SCCS files to which it is an interface. The group ID for the command is to be the read permission group for the SCCS files. The mode of the command is to be 4710. Thus, the SCCS file owner or group will acquire an effective UID of the owner of the SCCS files.

If the full SCCS file path name is not provided, the **sfint{xx}** will construct the full path name from the environmental variables SDIR (SCCS directory), WDIR (working directory), and CDIR (current working directory). These variables can be set by the **setsfm** command described in Appendix F.

Options

   -C All the SCCS commands described above plus the **admin -t** command (see **dted** command in Appendix F) can be executed without having to be linked as a separate command. This option is provided to encourage the use of the special shell scripts and to reduce the number of commands that need to be created. Thus, the following two commands are equivalent:

> sfintsfm -Cget s.sfint.c
> getsfm s.sfint.c

All other options are as specified for the particular SCCS command. The **sfint{xx}** program will pass the arguments to the command without changes.

Example

1. It is assumed that all commands exist in the directory /usr/sfm and that the user's PATH has been modified to include this directory. The following commands can then be used to create the necessary SCCS interface commands for a product called **cc**:

> $ cp /usr/sfm/sfintxx /usr/sfm/sfintcc
> $ chown clang /usr/sfm/sfintcc
> $ chgrp cgrp /usr/sfm/sfintcc
> $ chmod 4710 /usr/sfm/sfintcc
> $ ln /usr/sfm/sfintcc /usr/sfm/cdccc

2. For the following examples, assume that execution of the **setsfm** command (see Appendix F) has set the following environmental variables:

> PSID = 1.2
> SDIR = /srclib/cc
> WDIR = /usr/myacct/cc

Given the above environment, the following are a few examples of how **sfint{xx}** could be used:

> $ sfintcc -Cget -e s.parse.c
> $ sgetcc -e s.parse.c
> $ sunget /srclib/cc/clib/s.parse.c

Source

Note: The line numbers shown below are not part of the actual SCCS program. They are included in the source listing only for purposes of reference.

```
1  /* sfint.c - SCCS Command Interface program */
2  /* Copyright 1989.  All Rights Reserved. */
3  /* Uniware Ltd. */
4
5  /* performs a setuid and setgid to the owner
6     and group IDs of this program.  This program
7     provides an interface for the get, delta, unget
8     rmdel, cdc, and the "admin -t" commands.
9  */
10
11 #include <stdio.h>
12 #include <sys/types.h>
13 #include <string.h>
14
15 #define USAGE"\
16 usage: getxx [options] {SCCS File name}\n\
17        deltaxx [options] {SCCS File name}\n\
18        cdcxx [options] {SCCS File name}\n\
19        rmdelxx -r{SID} {SCCS File name}\n\
20        ungetxx [options] {SCCS File name}\n\
21        where xx is the product name.\n"
22
23 #define ADMERR "ERROR: Only -t option allowed with  admin\n"
24 #define NOSDIR "ERROR: Unknown SCCS Directory\n"
25 #define NOWDIR "ERROR: Unknown Work Directory\n"
26 #define NOCDIR "ERROR: Unknown Current Working  Directory\n"
27
28 #define ERET1 1
29 #define TRUE 1
30 #define FALSE 0
31 #define MAXCMD 7
32 #define PATHLEN 64
33
34 char    sccsid[] = "%W% %F% %Y% %D% %Q%";
35
36 /* SCCS Command List */
37
38 char    *cdir = "/usr/bin/";
39 char    *vcmd[] = {"sfint","get","delta","unget","rmdel","cdc","admin" };
40 int     aflag = FALSE;
41
42 /* Variable Definition */
43
44 char    **nargv;
45 void    appath(), exit(), perror(), substr();
46
47 main(argc, argv, envp)
48 int     argc;
```

```
49 char      **argv, **envp;
50 {
51          int     i, j;
52          char    *path;
53          char    tmp1[PATHLEN];
54          nargv = (char **)calloc((unsigned)argc, sizeof (char **));
55
56          if (argc < 2 || (i = chkcmd(argc, argv)) == 0) {
57                  fprintf(stderr,USAGE);
58                  exit (ERET1);
59          }
60          nargv[0] = vcmd[i];
61          strcat((path = cdir), vcmd[i]);
62          if (strcmp(vcmd[i], "admin") == 0) aflag = TRUE;
63          j = 1;
64          for (i = 1; i < argc; i++) {
65                  if (*argv[i] == '-') switch (argv[i][1]) {
66                  case 'C':
67                      continue;
68                  case 't':
69                      nargv[j++] = argv[i];
70                      continue;
71                  default :
72                          if (aflag == TRUE) {
73                                  fprintf(stderr,ADMERR);
74                                  exit (ERET1);
75                          }
76                          nargv[j++] = argv[i];
77                          continue;
78                  }
79                  else if (*argv[i] == '/') nargv[j++] = argv[i];
80                  else if (*argv[i] != '\0') {
81                          strcpy(tmp1, argv[i]);
82                          appath(tmp1);
83                          nargv[j++] = tmp1;
84                  }
85          }
86          nargv[j] = NULL;
87          execve(path, nargv, envp);
88          fprintf(stderr, "ERROR: cannot execute %s", path);
89          exit (ERET1);
90 }
91
92 /* Check for valid command */
93
94 int chkcmd(narg, targ)
95 int     narg;
96 char    **targ;
97 {
98          int     i;
99          char    *j, *tmpc;
100
101          j = strrchr(targ[0], '\/');
102          tmpc = (j == 0) ? targ[0] : ++j;
103          if (strncmp(tmpc, "sfint", 5) == 0) {
104                  for (i = 1; i < narg; i++) {
```

```
105                               if (*targ[i] == '-' && targ[i][1] == 'C')
106                                     tmpc = &targ[i][2];
107                         }
108               }
109               for (i = 1; i < MAXCMD; i++) {
100                         if (!strncmp(tmpc, vcmd[i], (strlen(vcmd[i]))))
110                                 return(i);
112               }
113               return(0);
114 }
115
116 /* Append SCCS and Component portions of path */
117
118 void appath(sfile)
119 char      *sfile;
120 {
121       char      *getenv(), *getcwd(), *sdir, *wdir, *cwd;
122       char      cmpnt[PATHLEN];
123       char      tname[PATHLEN];
124
125       if ((sdir = getenv("SDIR")) == NULL) {
126               fprintf(stderr,NOSDIR);
127               exit (ERET1);
128       }
129       if ((wdir = getenv("WDIR")) == NULL) {
130               fprintf(stderr,NOWDIR);
131               exit (ERET1);
132       }
133       if ((cwd = getenv("CDIR")) == NULL) {
134               fprintf(stderr,NOCDIR);
135               exit (ERET1);
136       }
137       substr(cmpnt, cwd, (strlen(wdir)), (strlen(cwd)));
138       sprintf(tname, "%s%s\/%s", sdir, cmpnt, sfile);
139       strcpy(sfile, tname);
140 }
141
142 /* Select a substring from str2 starting at bpos to epos
143  * and put results int str1.
144  */
145
146 void substr(str1, str2, bpos, epos)
147 char      *str1, *str2;
148 int       bpos, epos;
149 {
150       int      i, j;
151
152       if (epos <= bpos)
153               str1[0] = '\0';
154       else {
155               j = 0;
156               for (i = bpos; i < epos; i++)
157                       str1[j++] = str2[i];
158               str1[j] = '\0';
159       }
160 }
```

Discussion

As mentioned above, **sfint{xx}** can be executed as either sfint{xx} or as one of the valid commands. The chkcmd function (line 94) verifies that the command name is valid. If the command was executed as sfint{xx}, then the -C option must be present; it provides the name for the command to be executed. If the command is valid, the chkcmd function will return the index to the command. This information is used to define the necessary variables for the exec system call.

Lines 63 through 85 process the contents of argv. The -C option is bypassed, and only the -t option is allowed for the **admin** command (see the **dted** command in Appendix F). All other options are passed to the output argv (nargv). If a file name is encountered, a check is made to see whether or not the SCCS pathname must be added. If the pathname is required, the appath subroutine (line 118) adds the SCCS path to the file name. To do this, the routine assumes that the source file is to be in, or is in, the current working directory (the same rule applies when using the SCCS commands). By subtracting the WDIR path from the path for the current working directory (as defined by CDIR), a relative path is found. The relative path is then added to the SDIR path to create the SCCS path. If any one of the variables CDIR, SDIR, or WDIR is not defined, the subroutine will fail.

The name of the current working directory must be passed to the interface program. It is possible that, as a result of being SUID, use of the "getcwd" function will fail because the owner of the sfint{xx} does not have search permission for the current path. This is especially true when the work source tree is in a directory that is owned by a user other than the owner of the product and the **newgrp** command is used to change the GID to the ID of the group that has read permission in the source library.

Additional Tools

TABLE F.1 OWNERSHIPS AND PERMISSIONS FOR TOOLS

Name	Owner	Group	Permission
deltast	sfm	sfm	755
dted	sfm	sfm	755
getst	sfm	sfm	755
pvinit	sfm	sfm	755
sdelta	sfm	sfm	755
setsfm	sfm	sfm	755
sfinit	sfm	sfm	755
sfintxx	Note 1	Note 2	4710
sget	sfm	sfm	755
srmdel	sfm	sfm	755
sunget	sfm	sfm	755
verst	sfm	sfm	755

Notes:

1. The owner must be the owner of the SCCS files to be accessed. See Appendix E for complete details.

2. The group must be the name of the group that has read permission to the SCCS files identified by note 1.

3. The execute permission for others must always be denied in sfintxx. The reason is that whoever has permission to execute this program will acquire an effective UID that is the same as the UID of the owner of the program. See Chapter 10 for a discussion of the security issues.

4. The following scripts are based on the rule that the name of the product directory in the source library is same as the {xx} suffix for the sfintxx command and is also the prefix for the product version file. For example, if the above programs were part of a product identified as sfm, the following names would be used:

/srclib/sfm	SCCS source tree
sfintsfm	SCCS command interface
sfm.pv	Product version file

5. It is recommended that all the programs exist in a directory called /usr/sfm. Only the source administrator should have write permission in this directory.

Name

deltast   Delta any open files in work source tree.

Syntax

deltast [-y{comment}] [-m{mrlist}] [-n]

Description

The primary function of this command is to delta the product version file (if it has been retrieved for edit). However, prior to deltaing the product version file, the work source tree is searched to verify that no other source files are still waiting to be deltaed. If any such files are found, a query is written to standard output as to whether or not the file should be deltaed. If a positive response is given, then the source file is deltaed with only the **-n** option being passed to the **sdelta** command. Once the entire work source tree has been checked, the product version file is deltaed using the comments and MR numbers given on the command line.

This command will use the parameters specified in the .sfmdata file (see the **getst** command). As a result, it must be executed from within the domain of the work source tree.

Options

-**y** Comment for product version file. If not entered on the command line, a prompt will be issued by the **delta** command for the comment.

-**m** The MR numbers for the product version file. As with the comment line, if the MR numbers are not entered and are required, they will be requested.

-**n** The default delta action is to delete the file that has been deltaed. This option will retrieve the SID that has just been deltaed. By retrieving a new copy of the source file, the ID keywords are expanded. This function of the -n option is different than the function of -n option for the **delta** command. The **delta** command does not delete the file, which means the ID keyword strings are still in the unexpanded form. This difference is especially important when the product is to be built after the deltas have been made. With the deltast command, the ID keywords are in the proper format for the **what** command.

Example

$ **deltast -y"comment line" -mmr001**

Source

Note: Throughout Appendix F, the line numbers shown are not part of the actual SCCS program. They are included in the source listing only for purposes of reference.

```
 1 :
 2 # %W% %F% %Y% %D% %Q%
 3
 4 # deltast - delta Work Source Tree into SCCS Source Tree
 5
 6 USAGE="\
 7 usage: deltast [-y{comment}] [-m{mrlist}] [-n]"
 8
 9 # Exit Codes and their meanings
10 # 0 - Normal
11 # 1 - Error Return
12
13 ERET1=1
14
15 # Temporary file Definitions
16 TMP1=/usr/tmp/$$dst1
17
18 # Variable Definitions
19 DELTA='sfint$PROD -Cdelta'
20 GET='sfint$PROD -Cget'
21 YOPT=
22 MOPT=
23 KEEP=
24 PATH=/bin:/usr/bin:/etc:/usr/sfm
25
26 # Interrupt trap
27 trap "rm -f /usr/tmp/$$*" 0 1 2 3 15
28
29 # process options
30
31 for ARG in "$@"
32 do
33   case "$ARG" in
34     -m*)  MOPT=\'$ARG\'
35           ;;
36     -n)   KEEP=$ARG
37           ;;
38     -y*)  YOPT=\'$ARG\'
39           ;;
40     -\?|\?|*)
41           echo "$USAGE" 1>&2
42           exit $ERET1
43           ;;
44   esac
45 done
46
47 # perform validation checks
48
```

```
49  . /usr/sfm/setsfm
50
51  # get Real User Name
52  eval `id | sed 's/[^(]*(\([^)]*\)).*/RUID="\1"/'`
53
54  # Check the Work Source Tree for open deltas
55
56  (cd $SDIR; find . -name p.* -print > $TMP1)
57  exec 3< $TMP1
58  exec 4<&0
59  exec 0<&3
60  while read PFILE
61  do
62    SFILE=`echo \`basename $PFILE\` | sed 's/^p/s/'`
63    WFILE=`echo $SFILE | sed 's/..//'`
64    CMPNT=`echo \`dirname $PFILE\` | sed 's/..//'`
65    SPATH=$SDIR/$CMPNT/$SFILE
66    WPATH=$WDIR/$CMPNT/$WFILE
67    if [ "$SFILE" != "s.$PROD.pv" -a -w "$WPATH" ]
68    then
69      exec 0<&4
70      ANS=
71      until [ "$ANS" = "y" -o "$ANS" = "n" ]
72      do
73        echo "$SPATH:"
74        sact $SPATH
75        echo "delta this file [ y or n ]? "\\c
76        read ANS
77      done
78      if [ $ANS = "y" ]
79      then
80        (CDIR=$WDIR/$CMPNT; cd $CDIR; sdelta $KEEP $SPATH)
81        if [ $? -ne 0 ]
82        then
83          exit $?
84        fi
85      else
86        echo "ERROR: All source files must be deltaed before"
87        echo "        the Product Version file can be deltaed."
88        exit $ERET1
89      fi
90      exec 0<&3
91    fi
92  done
93  exec 0<&4
94
95  # once the source files in the Work Source Tree have been
96  # deltaed the Product Version File can be deltaed.
97  SPATH=$SDIR/prod/s.$PROD.pv
98  echo "$SPATH:"
99  NSID=`sact $SPATH 2> /dev/null | grep "$DSID.*$RUID" | awk '{print $2}'`
100 if (CDIR=$WDIR/prod; cd $CDIR; \
101     eval $DELTA -r$PSID $MOPT $YOPT $SPATH)
102 then
103   sed /PSID/s/$PSID/$NSID/ < $WDIR/.sfmdata > $TMP1
```

```
104    cp $TMP1 $WDIR/.sfmdata
105    if [ -n "$KEEP" ]
106    then
107      (CDIR=$WDIR/prod; cd $CDIR; eval $GET -r$NSID -s $SPATH)
108    fi
109 fi
```

Discussion

The DELTA and GET variables (lines 19 and 20) are used to define the delta and get commands to be used.

Lines 29 through 45 form the routine for processing the arguments. Since the MOPT and YOPT arguments may contain white space, they have to be quoted. Moreover, the quotes have to be retained for the eval command (line 101).

All environmental validation checks are performed by the **setsfm** script (line 49). Line 52 extracts the real user name from the output of the **id** command. The real user name is used as part of the **p-file** search in line 99.

Line 56 is used to build a list of all the **p-file**s in the SCCS source tree for the product. Lines 57 through 93 constitute the routine that processes this list of **p-file**s. The assumption is that a **p-file** plus a corresponding **g-file** in the work source tree means the file needs to be deltaed. If the answer to the query is positive, then the **sdelta** command is called to delta the source file. A negative answer will terminate the **deltast** command. To keep the product version file in sync, all open deltas must be completed before deltaing the product version file.

Lines 95 through 101 are used to delta the product version file. Lines 103 through 104 update the .sfmdata file with the new SID for the product version file. Lines 105 through 108 will retrieve a new copy of the product version file if the **-n** option is given.

Note: Line 24 explicitly declares the PATH. This is done to ensure that a "trojan horse" is not substituted for the real **sfint{xx}** program. This practice is followed by all the shell scripts in this appendix that execute **sfint{xx}**.

_____

Name

            dted   Edit Descriptive Text of an SCCS file.

Syntax

           dted [-e{name of editor}] {file ...}

Description

The purpose of this command is to edit the descriptive text section of an SCCS file. To do this, the command must perform the following tasks:

1. The ID of the user executing the command is validated against the information in the user table. If it is not a valid UID, then the command will be aborted.

2. If it is available, the existing descriptive text will be retrieved into a temporary file.

3. Either the default editor or the editor specified on the command line will be invoked to allow editing of the temporary file.

4. The resulting temporary file will replace the existing descriptive text in the SCCS file.

The argument {file . . .} may specify an SCCS file or several SCCS files, or, if not entered, it will default to all SCCS files for the current component.

Options

-e The default is to invoke **ed** as the editor. A different editor can be invoked by specifying the name of the editor as the argument to the -e option.

Example

```
$ dted s.journal.cob
$ dted -evi s.journal.cob
```

Source

```
1 :
2 # %W% %F% %Y% %D% %Q%
3
4 # dted - Edit Descriptive Text of an SCCS File
5
6 USAGE="usage: dted [-e{name of editor}] {SCCS File ...}"
7
8 # Exit Codes and their meanings
9 # 0 - Normal
10 # 1 - Error
11
12 ERET1=1
13
14 # Temporary file Definitions
15 TMP1=/usr/tmp/$$dt1
16
17 # Variable Definitions
18 ADMIN='sfint$PROD -Cadmin'
19 SFILE=
20 STMP=
21 PATH=/bin:/usr/bin:/etc:/usr/sfm
22
23 # Interrupt trap
```

```
24  trap "rm -f /usr/tmp/$$*" 0 1 2 3 15
25
26  # process the options
27
28  for ARG in "$@"
29  do
30    case "$ARG" in
31      -e*) EDITOR=`echo $ARG | sed 's/..//'`
32           ;;
33      -\?|\?)
34             echo $USAGE 1>&2
35             exit $ERET1
36             ;;
37      *)     SFILE="$SFILE""$ARG "
38             ;;
39    esac
40  done
41
42  # perform validations checks
43
44  . /usr/sfm/setsfm
45
46  # get real user id
47  eval `id | sed 's/[^(]*(\([^)]*\)).*/RUID="\1"/'`
48
49  # The following lines are used to determine the Relative
50  # Path name (RPATH), which is equal to CDIR-WDIR.
51  RPATH=`eval basename \`pwd\``
52  WPATH=`eval dirname \`pwd\``
53  until [ "$WDIR" = "$WPATH" -o "$WPATH" = '/']
54  do
55  RPATH=`basename $WPATH`"/$RPATH"
56  WPATH=`dirname $WPATH`
57  done
58  if [ "$WPATH" = '/' ]
59  then
60    echo "ERROR: $WDIR not a valid directory." 1>&2
61    exit $ERET1
62  fi
63
64  # if no files are specified, use files in current working directory
65  if [ -z "$SFILE" ]
66  then
67    for I in *
68      do
69        SFILE="$SFILE""s.$I "
70    done
71  fi
72
73  # now edit the Descriptive Text Portion of the SCCS File
74  for I in $SFILE
75  do
76
77    # if necessary, convert to absolute SCCS path name
78    if [ `expr "$I" : '\(.\)'` \| 'x'` = "/" ]
```

```
79    then
80      SPATH=$I
81    else
82      SPATH=$SDIR/$RPATH/$I
83    fi
84
85    # edit the file
86    echo "$SPATH":
87    if val -s $SPATH
88    then
89      if (prs -d:UN: $SPATH | grep $RUID 1> /dev/null 2>&1) &&
90        (prs -d:FD: $SPATH | sed '$d' > $TMP1)
91      then
92        ${EDITOR:=ed} $TMP1
93        eval $ADMIN -t$TMP1 $SPATH
94      else
95        echo "ERROR: $RUID does not have delta permission." 1>&2
96      fi
97    else
98      echo "$SPATH: Not an SCCS File"
99    fi
100 done
```

Discussion

The variable ADMIN in line 18 defines the interface to the **admin** command.

All the validation and setting of environmental variables is performed by the **setsfm** script described in this appendix.

The real UID is obtained in line 47. The RUID will be compared against the UID in the user table for each SCCS file processed in line 89.

Lines 51 through 62 determine the relative PATH (RPATH) for the current working directory. If no files were specified, lines 65 through 71 will build a list of SCCS files for each file in the current working directory.

For each file defined, lines 78 through 83 will create an absolute path to the SCCS file if one was not provided. If this is a valid SCCS file (line 87), the user table is searched for a match with the RUID. The descriptive text is retrieved into a work file (line 90). If these steps are successfully executed, the file is edited using the editor specified or the default editor, **ed**. The revised text is then returned to the SCCS file by use of **admin**.

Note: The user validation routine does not include the possibility that the user table could be empty. The basic premise is that the security procedures described in Chapter 10 are being followed.

Name

getst   Retrieve SCCS source tree into work source tree.

Syntax

> getst [-r{prod SID}] [-c{component list}]
> [-w{work path}] [-t] [-s{SCCS path}]

Description

The **getst** command builds the work source tree in the current working directory or the directory defined by **-w{work path}**. The model for the work source tree is the SCCS source tree as defined by the option **-s{SCCS path}**. The complete work source tree is built unless **-c{component list}** is specified. If the **{component list}** is given, then the work source tree structure will be created only to the extent needed to retrieve those components plus the **prod** directory. If no **-r{prod SID}** is given, then the product version file with SID of **mR.mL** is retrieved. By using the **-r** option, any version of the product version file can be retrieved. The versions of the source files retrieved are defined by the SIDs specified in the product version file.

To support the other local tools, a file with the name of **".sfmdata"** is created in the {work path}/{prod} directory. The variable {prod} is the basename of the SCCS path and is used to define the name of the product. The contents of this file are as follows:

> SDIR = {SCCS path}; export SDIR
> WDIR = {work path}; export WDIR
> PSID = {prod SID}; export PSID

If the SDIR environmental variable is currently defined, then the **-s** option does not need to be entered. The WDIR and PSID environmental variables are ignored by the **getst** command.

Options

-c This option is used when only selected components are to be retrieved. The tree structure created will be the minimal necessary to support the component list. The **prod** directory is always created, since it contains the product version file that is required to retrieve the source files for the specified components. The **{component list}** may contain one or more components separated by a space or tab character. A list with multiple components must be enclosed in quotes.

-r This option is used to specify the SID of the product version file to be the base for the retrieving of source files. If the delta defined by **{prod SID}** does not exist for the product version file, the command will be aborted. The default is to use the SID specified by **mR.mL** *Note:* This may be altered by changing the default SID for the SCCS file of the product version file.

-s Unless the SDIR environmental variable is defined, the **-s{SCCS path}** option must be entered. This option specifies the product directory to be used for retrieving the work source tree from the SCCS source tree. The basename of the {**SCCS path**} is used to define the product name for retrieving the product version file and for identifying the SCCS interface command.

-t This option suppresses the actual retrieval of the source files, including the product version file.

-w The default is to define the current working directory as the {work path}. If a different directory is to be used, then it must be specified by using the **-w{work path}** option. The {work path} argument may be a relative pathname as well as a fully qualified pathname.

Examples

```
$ getst -s/srclib/gl
$ getst -r1.4 -s/srclib/gl
$ getst -r1.4 -cjrnl -s/srclib/gl
$ getst -r1.4 -c"jrnl cmngl" -s/srclib/gl
$ getst -r1.5 -w/usr/myacct -s/srclib/gl
$ getst -w/usr/myacct -t -s/srclib/gl
```

Source

```
1  :
2  # %W% %F% %Y% %D% %Q%
3
4  # getst - Retrieve SCCS Source into Work Source Tree
5
6  USAGE="\
7  usage: getst [-r{prod SID}] [-c{component list}]
8          [-w{work path}] [-t] [-s{SCCS path}]"
9
10 # Exit Codes and their meanings
11 # 0 - Normal
12 # 1 - Error Return
13
14 ERET1=1
15
16 # Temporary file Definitions
17 TMP1=/usr/tmp/$$gst1
18 TMP2=/usr/tmp/$$gst2
19
20 # Variable Definitions
21 PSID=
22 WDIR=
23 CLIST=
24 TFLAG=1
25
26 # Interrupt trap
27 trap "rm -f /usr/tmp/$$*" 0 1 2 3 15
28
29 # process options
```

```
30
31 for ARG in "$@"
32 do
33   case "$ARG" in
34     -r*) PSID=`echo $ARG | sed 's/..//'`
35          ;;
36     -c*) CLIST=`echo $ARG | sed 's/..//'`
37          ;;
38     -w*) WDIR=`echo $ARG | sed 's/..//'`
39          ;;
40     -s*) SDIR=`echo $ARG | sed 's/..//'`
41          ;;
42     =t)  TFLAG=0
43          ;;
44     -\?\?|*)
45            echo "$USAGE" 1>&2
46            exit $ERET1
47            ;;
48   esac
49 done
50
51 # perform validation checks
52
53 if [ -z "$SDIR" ]
54 then
55   echo "ERROR: SCCS Directory not defined." 1>&2
56   exit $ERET1
57 fi
58 if [ ! -d "$SDIR" ]
59 then
60   echo "ERROR: $SDIR not a valid directory." 1>&2
61   exit $ERET1
62 fi
63 if [ ! -r "$SDIR" ]
64 then
65   echo "ERROR: $SDIR read permission denied." 1>&2
66   exit $ERET1
67 fi
68 if [ ! -d "$SDIR/prod" ]
69 then
70   echo "ERROR: $SDIR not a product directory." 1>&2
71   exit $ERET1
72 fi
73
74 # Product Version File and PSID validation
75 PROD=`basename $SDIR`
76 if val -s $SDIR/prod/s.$PROD.pv
77 then
78   if [ -z "$PSID" ]
79   then
80     PSID=`get -g $SDIR/prod/s.$PROD.pv`
81   else
82     if get -r$PSID -g $SDIR/prod/s.$PROD.pv > $TMP1
83     then
84       PSID=`cat $TMP1`
```

```
85   else
86       echo "ERROR: $PSID not a valid SID." 1>&2
87       exit $ERET1
88     fi
89   fi
90 else
91   echo "ERROR: valid Product Version File not found." 1>&2
92   exit $ERET1
93 fi
94
95 # Validate base of Work Source Tree
96 WDIR=${WDIR:-`pwd`}
97 if [ ! -d "$WDIR" ]
98 then
99   echo "ERROR: $WDIR not a valid directory." 1>&2
100   exit $ERET1
101 fi
102
103 # Build the Work Source Tree
104 if [ `basename "$WDIR"` != $PROD ]
105 then
106   if [ ! -d "$WDIR/$PROD" ]
107   then
108     mkdir -m 770 $WDIR/$PROD
109   fi
110   WDIR=$WDIR/$PROD
111 fi
112 if [ ! -d "$WDIR/prod" ]
113 then
114   mkdir -m 770 $WDIR/prod
115 fi
116 if [ $TFLAG -ne 0 ]
117 then
118   cd $WDIR/prod
119   get -r$PSID -s $SDIR/prod/s.$PROD.pv
120   PVF=$WDIR/prod/$PROD.pv
121 fi
122
123 # get list of directories from SCCS Source Tree
124 cd $SDIR
125 find . -type d -print > $TMP1
126 cd $WDIR
127
128 # if there is a component list, /use only/ those components
129 if [ ! -z "$CLIST" ]
130 then
131   for CMPNT in $CLIST
132   do
133     grep $CMPNT $TMP1 >> $TMP2
134   done
135   mv $TMP2 $TMP1
136 fi
137
138 # based on the list of directories defined above, build
139 # the equivalent Work Source Tree
```

```
140 exec 3< $TMP1
141 exec 0<&3
142 while read CDIR
143 do
144    CDIR=`echo $CDIR | sed 's/..//'`
145    CMPNT=`basename "$CDIR"`
146
147 # for a component to be added it must exist in the
        Product Version File
148    if (grep "^$CMPNT" $PVF 1> /dev/null 2>&1)
149    then
150      cd $WDIR
151      if [ ! -d "$CDIR" ]
152      then
153        mkdir -m 770 -p $CDIR
154      fi
155
156 # if the source files are to be retrieved, use
        the Product Version
157 # File for names and SIDs of files to be retrieved.
158      if [ $TFLAG -ne 0 ]
159      then
160        cd $WDIR/$CDIR
161        awk "\$1 == \"$CMPNT\" { print \$2, \$3 }" $PVF >> $TMP2
162        exec 4< $TMP2
163        exec 0<&4
164        while read SFILE FSID
165        do
166          get -r$FSID -s $SDIR/$CDIR/$SFILE
167        done
168        rm -f $TMP2
169        exec 0<&3
170      fi
171    fi
172 done
173
174 # build the sfmdata file
175 cd $WDIR
176 cat > .sfmdata <<-EOF
177        SDIR=$SDIR; export SDIR
178        WDIR=$WDIR; export WDIR
179        PSID=$PSID; export PSID
180        EOF
181 chmod 750 $WDIR/.sfmdata
```

Discussion

This script must independently validate the environment (lines 51 through
101), since the .sfmdata file required by the **setsfm** is created as the last step
of this script.

The first step in building the work source tree is to build the **prod** directory
and, depending on whether or not the **-t** option was entered, to retieve the

product version file (lines 104 through 121). To create the work source tree, the tree structure of the SCCS source tree is written to a temporary file (see line 125). If a component list has been specified, then only those components are selected (lines 129 through 136).

Lines 140 though 173 build the work source tree based on the directory list created above. In lines 158 through 170, the source files for the component are retrieved if the **-t** option has not been entered.

The section defined by lines 175 through 181 builds the .sfmdata file in the directory defined by WDIR.

Name

pvinit   Initialize the product version file.

Syntax

pvinit [{SCCS Path}]

Description

The **pvinit** command searches the product directory for all SCCS files. For each SCCS file that it finds, an entry in the product version file is created. Non-SCCS files and files without read permission are ignored.

If the {**SCCS Path**} is not specified, **pvinit** checks to see if it can find the **prod** directory in the current working directory. If it does, the current working directory is taken to be the {**SCCS Path**}.

The script will create a file called <**prod**>**.pv** in the **prod** directory, where <**prod**> is the basename of the {**SCCS Path**}.

Options

There are no options to the **pvinit** command.

Examples

$ pvinit /srclib/gl
$ pvinit

Source

```
1 :
2 # %W% %F% %Y% %D% %Q%
3
4 # pvinit - Initialize the Product Version File
5
```

```
 6 USAGE="usage: pvinit [{product directory}]"
 7
 8 # Exit Codes and their meanings
 9 # 0 - Normal
10 # 1 - Error Return
11
12 ERET1=1
13
14 # Temporary file Definitions
15 TMP1=/usr/tmp/$$pvt
16
17 # Variable Definitions
18 PDIR=`pwd`
19
20 # interrupt trap
21 trap "rm -f /usr/tmp/$$*" 0 1 2 3 15
22
23 # test for options
24
25 if [ "$#" -gt 1 ]
26 then
27    echo $USAGE 1>&2
28    exit $ERET1
29 fi
30
31 for ARG in "$@"
32 do
33    case "$ARG" in
34      -\?|\?)
35          echo $USAGE 1>&2
36          exit $ERET1
37          ;;
38      *) if [ -d "$ARG" ]
39          then
40             PDIR="$ARG"
41             cd $PDIR
42          else
43             echo "ERROR: Invalid Product Directory." 1>&2
44             exit $ERET1
45          fi
46    esac
47 done
48
49 # Check if in correct directory
50
51 if [ -d "$PDIR/prod" ]
52 then
53    true
54 else
55    echo "ERROR: $PDIR/prod not found." 1>&2
56    exit $ERET1
57 fi
58
59 # build a list of the SCCS Files
60
```

```
61 PROD='basename $PDIR`
62 echo '#' \%W\% \%F\% \%Y\% \%D\% \%Q\% | cat >\
      $PDIR/prod/$PROD.pv
63 find "$PDIR" -name s.* -exec val -s {} \; \
64      -exec prs -r -d":M: :F: :I:" {} >> $TMP1 \;
65 sort $TMP1 >> $PDIR/prod/$prod.pv
```

Discussion

This is a very simple shell script. Once all the edit checks have been made, the product version file is created in lines 61 through 65.

Note: This shell scripts works correctly only if the **m** (module name) flag in the SCCS file is set to the component name. This should not be a problem if the **sfinit** command was used to build the SCCS files.

Name

        sdelta   Special version of the delta command.

Syntax

        sdelta [delta command options] {SCCS File . . .}

Description

The **sdelta** command is a front-end to the **sfint{xx} -Cdelta** command. As such, it performs the following functions:

1. It collects the options for the **delta** command. With the exception of the **-n** option, all the options entered are passed to the **delta** command.
2. The argument {file . . .} may specify an SCCS file or several SCCS files, or, if not entered, it will default to all the SCCS files in the current working directory. The path name for the SCCS file(s) is determined from the environmental variables SDIR and WDIR, plus the component name for the source file.
3. The **-n** option is not passed to the **delta** command. Instead, after the delta has been made, the file, which was removed by the **delta** command, is retrieved from the SCCS file. This approach will force the ID keyword strings to be expanded.
4. If the **delta** command is successful, the SID in the product version file for the source file is changed to the value of the delta SID.

> **Warning!** This command only updates the product version file. Once all
> changes to the product have been completed, the product version file
> must be deltaed. Failure to delta the product version file can cause prob-
> lems when retrieving the product for the next round of updates.

Options

With the exception of the **-n** (see above) option, the options are the same as
those for the **delta** command.

Examples

$ sdelta s.journal.cob
$ sdelta -y"a comment line" -mmr001 s.journal.cob

Source

```
1 :
2 # %W% %F% %Y% %D% %Q%
3
4 # sdelta - delta command interface
5
6 USAGE="usage: sdelta [delta command options] {SCCS File ...}"
7
8 # Exit Codes and their meanings
9 # 0 - Normal
10 # 1 - Error
11
12 ERET1=1
13
14 # Variable Definitions
15 CMDL=
16 GET='sfint$PROD -Cget'
17 DELTA='sfint$PROD -Cdelta'
18 DSID=
19 MOPT=
20 PROD=
21 SFILE=
22 YOPT=
23 KEEP=1
24 PATH=/bin:/usr/bin:/etc:/usr/sfm
25
26 # process the options
```

```
27
28  for ARG in "$@"
29  do
30    case "$ARG" in
31      -m*)  MOPT=\'$ARG\'
32            ;;
33       -n)  KEEP=0
34            ;;
35      -r*)  DSID=`echo $ARG | sed 's/..//'`
36            CMDL="$CMDL""$ARG "
37            ;;
38      -y*)  YOPT=\'$ARG\'
39            ;;
40      -\?|\?)
41            echo $USAGE 1>&2
42            exit $ERET1
43            ;;
44      -*)   CMDL="$CMDL""$ARG "
45            ;;
46       *)   SFILE="$SFILE""$ARG "
47            ;;
48    esac
49  done
50
51  # perform validations checks
52  . /usr/sfm/setsfm
53  if [ ! -w *$WDIR/prod/$PROD.pv" ]
54  then
55    echo "WARNING: Product Version File cannot be updated." 1>&2
56  fi
57
58  # get the real user name
59  eval `id | sed 's/[^(]*(\([^)]*\)).*/RUID="\1"/'`
60
61  # The following lines are used to determine the Relative
62  # Path name (RPATH), which is equal to CDIR - WDIR.
63  RPATH=`eval basename \`pwd\``
64  WPATH=`eval dirname \`pwd\``
65  until [ "$WDIR" = "$WPATH" -o "$WPATH" = '/' ]
66  do
67    RPATH=`basename $WPATH`"/$RPATH"
68    WPATH=`dirname $WPATH`
69  done
70  if [ "$WPATH" = '/' ]
71  then
72    echo "ERROR: $WDIR not a valid directory." 1>&2
73    exit $ERET1
74  fi
75
76  # if no files specified, delta all files in current directory
77  if [ -z "$SFILE" ]
78  then
79    for I in *
80    do
81      SFILE="$SFILE""s.$I "
```

```
 82    done
 83 fi
 84
 85 # now execute a delta for each SCCS File defined
 86 for I in $SFILE
 87 do
 88
 89    # if necessary, add absolute SCCS pathname.
 90    if [ `expr "$I" : '\(.\)'`'\|' 'x'` = "/" ]
 91    then
 92      SPATH=$I
 93    else
 94      SPATH=$SDIR/$RPATH/$I
 95    fi
 96
 97    # delta the file
 98    echo "$SPATH":
 99    if val -s $SPATH
100    then
101      NSID=`sact $SPATH 2>/dev/null | grep "$DSID.*$RUID"\
             | awk '{print $2}'`
102      eval $DELTA $CMDL $MOPT $YOPT $SPATH
103      if val -s -r$NSID $SPATH
104      then
105        if [ -w "$WDIR/prod/$PROD.pv" ]
106        then
107          SNAME=`basename $SPATH`
108          CMPNT=`eval basename \`dirname $SPATH\``
109          ed -s $WDIR/prod/$PROD.pv <<-EOF
110          /$CMPNT $SNAME/c
111          $CMPNT $SNAME $NSID
112          .
113          w
114          q
115          EOF
116        fi
117        if [ $KEEP -eq 0 ]
118        then
119          eval $GET -r$NSID -s $SPATH
120        fi
121      fi
122    else
123      echo "$SPATH: Not a valid SCCS File"
124    fi
125 done
```

Discussion

If the **-r** option is entered, the delta SID is saved in the variable DSID (line 35). This variable and the RUID variable obtained in line 59 compose the elements for selecting the correct record from the p-file in line 101.

Lines 63 through 74 define the relative path name (RPATH). The variable

RPATH will define the path relative to WDIR. By adding RPATH to SDIR, the SCCS path is obtained.

If no files were specified on the command line, the routine defined in lines 77 through 83 will create a list SCCS files based on the source file names found in the current working directory.

All the files will then be deltaed in the routine defined in lines 86 through 125. As part of this routine, the product version file will be updated.

Name

setsfm   Set the product environment.

Syntax

setsfm

Description

Starting with the current working directory, the directories are searched in ascending order until the **.sfmdata** file is found. Based on the information in the .sfmdata file (see the **getst** command), the environmental variables **WDIR**, **SDIR**, and **PSID** are then set. As a precaution, the variables are checked to ensure that they are correct. The variable **PROD** is set to the basename of SDIR. Also, the variable **CDIR** is set to the current working directory.

Options

There are no options to this command.

Example

$. setsfm

Source

```
1  :
2  # %W% %F% %Y% %D% %Q%
3
4  # setsfm -Build environment for sfm scripts
5
6  # Variables to be exported to the environment
7  # SDIR = SCCS Directory
8  # WDIR = WORK Directory
9  # PSID = PSID
10 # PROD = PRODuct name
11 # CDIR = Current Working Directory
12
```

```
13 USAGE="usage: setsfm"
14
15 # Exit Codes and their meanings
16 # 0 - Normal
17 # 1 - Invalid environment
18
19 ERET1=1
20
21 # Check access permission to current working directory
22 if CDIR=`pwd 2> /dev/null`
23 then
24    true
25 else
26    echo "ERROR: Access permission to path denied." 1>&2
27    exit $ERET1
28 fi
29
30 # find .sfmdata file by checking each directory in reverse sequence
31 # of the path.
32 TDIR=$CDIR
33 while [ "$TDIR" != '/' ]
34 do
35    if [ -f "$TDIR/.sfmdata" ]
36    then
37       break
38    fi
39    TDIR=`dirname $TDIR`
40 done
41 if [ "$TDIR" = '/' ]
42 then
43    echo "ERROR: .sfmdata file not found in current path." 1>&2
44    exit $ERET1
45 fi
46
47 # establish environment based on .sfmdata
48
49  . $TDIR/.sfmdata
50
51 # validate environment
52
53 if [ -z "$SDIR" ]
54 then
55    echo "ERROR: SCCS Directory not defined." 1>&2
56    exit $ERET1
57 fi
58 if [ ! -d "$SDIR" ]
59 then
60    echo "ERROR: $SDIR not a valid directory." 1>&2
61    exit $ERET1
62 fi
63 if [ ! -r "$SDIR" ]
64 then
65    echo "ERROR: $SDIR read permission denied." 1>&2
66    exit $ERET1
67    fi
```

```
68 if [ ! -d "$SDIR/prod" ]
69 then
70   echo "ERROR: $SDIR not a product directory." 1>&2
71   exit $ERET1
72 fi
73 PROD=`basename $SDIR`
74 if [ "$TDIR" != "$WDIR" ]
75 then
76   echo "ERROR: $WDIR not a valid directory." 1>&2
77   exit $ERET1
78 fi
79 if [ -z "$PSID" ]
80 then
81   echo "ERROR: PSID not defined." 1>&2
82   exit $ERET1
83 fi
84
85 export SDIR WDIR PSID PROD CDIR
```

Discussion

The first task is to define CDIR (current working directory). If access permission is denied to the search path, the script will fail. The next task is to find the .sfmdata file, which is defined in lines 32 through 45. Starting with the current working directory and working up the tree, each directory is checked for the existence of the .sfmdata file. The search stops when the root directory is all that remains of the source tree.

Once the .sfmdata file has been found, it is executed to set the environmental variables (see line 49). In lines 53 through 83, the variables are validated to ensure that the environment has not changed. If nothing has changed, the variables are moved to the environment using **export**.

Name

sfinit   Initialize SCCS files.

Syntax

sfinit -p{prod} [-s] [-r{rel}] [-y{comment}]
[-m{mrlist}] [-a{login name}...]
[-f{flag}[{flag-val}]...] [-t{text file}]

Description

For every source file in a component, **sfinit** will create a SCCS file and load the first delta. Unless otherwise modified on the command line, the default actions are as follows:

1. The ID required (**i**) flag is set with "%W%" as the verification string.
2. The value for the **q** flag is the argument for the **-p** option.
3. The name of the current directory will be used as the value for the module name (**m**) flag.
4. The value of the module type (**t**) flag will default to the suffix of the file name. For example, the value for the file name exampl.c would be "c". If the file name does not have a suffix, the module type will be "unk".
5. Unless the **-s** option is specified, the source files will be removed as soon as the SCCS file is created.

The **-p{prod}** argument is required, and the argument {prod} must be the name of the product directory.

Options

-**s** This option suppresses the automatic deletion of the source files after the SCCS file has been created. This option should rarely be used, as deleting source files after the fact is very time consuming.

-**p** This option is required. It specifies the name of the product directory and is used as the argument for the **-q** flag.

* All the other options are the same as those for the **admin** command (see Chapter 4).

Example

$ **sfinit -r4 -mmr01 -y"initial delta" -apgmr1 -apgmr2** \
> **-fb -fvmrval -t/srclib/tmp/decrip.t -pgl**

Source

```
 1 :
 2 # %W% %F% %Y% %D% %Q%
 3
 4 # sfinit - Initialize SCCS Files
 5
 6 USAGE=\
 7 usage: sfinit -p{prod} [-s] [-r{rel}] [-y{comments}] [-m{mrlist}]
 8        [-a{login ID}...] [-f{flag}[{flag-val}]...] [-t{text file}]"
 9
10 # Exit Codes and their meanings
11 # 0 - Normal
12 # 1 - Error Return
13
14 ERET1=1
15
```

```
16  # Variable Definitions - By adding values to the following variable
17  # the default for the variable can be changed.
18
19  QFLAG=-fq
20  MFLAG=-fm
21  TFLAG=-ft
22  IFLAG=-fi\%W\%
23  VFLAG=
24  MOPT=
25  YOPT=
26  PROD=
27  CMDL=
28  TARG=
29  DELFILE=0
30
31  # test for required options
32
33  if test "$#" -lt 1
34  then
35      echo "$USAGE" 1>&2
36      exit $ERET1
37  fi
38
39  # Process command line
40
41  CNAME=`basename \`pwd\``
42  MFLAG="$MFLAG""$CNAME"
43  for ARGS in "$@"
44  do
45      case "$ARGS" in
46        -p*)  PROD=`echo $ARGS | sed 's/..//'`
47              QFLAG="$QFLAG""$PROD"
48              ;;
49        -s)   DELFILE=1
50              ;;
51        -m*)  MOPT=\'$ARGS\'
52              ;;
53        -f*)  case `echo $ARGS |sed 's/..//'` in
54                m*)  MFLAG=\'$ARGS\'
55                     ;;
56                i*)  IFLAG=\'$ARGS\'
57                     ;;
58                q*)  QFLAG=\'$ARGS\'
59                     ;;
60                t*)  TARG=\'$ARGS\'
61                     ;;
62                v*)  VFLAG=$ARGS
63                     ;;
64                b|n|j)
65                     CMDL="$CMDL""$ARGS "
66                     ;;
67                *) echo *ERROR: flag not valid for file initialization" 1>&2
68                     exit $ERET1
69                     ;;
70              esac
```

```
71              ;;
72      -y*)  YOPT=\'$ARGS\'
73              ;;
74      -r*|-a*|-t*)
75              CMDL="$CMDL""$ARGS "
76              ;;
77      -\?|\?)
78              echo "$USAGE" 1>&2
79              exit $ERET1
80              ;;
81      *)    echo "ERROR: Invalid Option - ""$ARGS" 1>&2
82              exit $ERET1
83              ;;
84    esac
85 done
86
87 # test for required options
88
89 if [ -z "$PROD" ]
90 then
91    echo "ERROR: -p option is required" 1>&2
92    exit $ERET1
93 fi
94
95 # Initialize files
96
97 for I in *
98 do
99    if [ -r "$I" -a `expr $I : '\(..\)'` != "s." ]
100    then
101      TARG=`expr $I : '.*\.\(.*\)'`
102      TFVAL="$TFLAG""${TARG:-unk}"
103      eval admin $CMDL $MFLAG $VFLAG $IFLAG $QFLAG \
104                  $TFVAL $YOPT $MOPT -i$I s.$I
105      if [ $? -eq 0 ]
106      then
107        echo "s.$I has been created." 1>&2
108        if [ $DELFILE -eq 0 ]
109        then
110          rm -f $I
111        fi
112      fi
113    fi
114 done
```

Discussion

Lines 19 through 25 define the default values for the variables used to initialize an SCCS file. Before changing the MFLAG variable, consider the impact on other shell scripts, which assume that it is set to the component name (for example, see pvinit above).

The version presented above is a generic version of the command. Repetitious typing of the options can be reduced by making a product-specific version of the command. All that is required to do this is to create variables for the default options. For example, the following lines could be added to the beginning of the script:

```
MOPT = -mmr001
PROD = GL
USERS = "-apgmr1 -apgmr2"
BFLAG = -fb
```

If the list of default variables is increased, any variables not currently defined on the admin command line (lines 103 and 104) need to be added.

Lines 41 through 85 are used to parse the command line. When parsing the **-f** option, a check is made to verify the flags that are being set. Only those flags that are valid for SCCS file initialization are allowed (see Chapter 4).

Lines 97 through 114 are used to create the SCCS file. The test on line 99 ensures that an SCCS file is not created for an existing SCCS file. Lines 101 and 102 determine the value for the module type **(t)** flag.

Name

      sget   Special **get** to support the product version file.

Syntax

      sget [get command options] {SCCS File ...}

Description

The **sget** command is essentially a preprocessor to the **sfint{xx} -Cget** command. As such, it performs the following functions:

1. It collects the arguments for the **get** command.
2. If the **-e** option is given and the product version file has not been retrieved for edit, a check will be made to verify that the SID for the product version file is a leaf SID. If it is not, **sget** will not process the request. If it is and the **get -e** is successful, the product version file is retrieved for edit. See Chapter 12 for an explanation of why this is necessary.
3. The default SID retrieved will be the SID specified in the product version file.
4. The argument {file . . .} can specify an SCCS file or several SCCS files, or, if no file is specified, all the SCCS files defined for the component in the product version file will be selected.
5. The actual path to the SCCS file need not be specified. The **sget** command will construct this path from information in the ".sfmdata" file.

Options

The options for the **sget** command are the same as for the **get** command. However, the **-r** option has a change in its syntax. The default SID for a source file is the SID specified in the product version file. This overrides both the default for the **get** command and the default SID (**d**) flag.

Examples

$ sget -e s.journal.cob	will get a single file and retrieve the product version file for updating.
$ sget -e -r1.5 s.journal.cob	will override the SID from the product version file.
$ sget -e	will get all the source files for the current component.

Source

```
 1 :
 2 # %W% %F% %Y% %D% %Q%
 3
 4 # sget - get command interface
 5
 6 USAGE="usage: sget [get command options] {SCCS File ...}"
 7
 8 # Exit Codes and their meanings
 9 # 0 - Normal
10 # 1 - Error
11
12 ERET1=1
13
14 # Temporary file Definitions
15 TMP1=/usr/tmp/$$dt1
16
17 # Variable Definitions
18 CMDL=
19 GET='sfint$PROD -Cget'
20 GETOK=1
21 GETPV=1
22 PROD=
23 SFILE=
24 STMP=
25 WOPT=
26 ROPT=
27 PATH=/bin:/usr/bin:/etc:/usr/sfm
28
29 # Interrupt trap
30 trap "rm -f /usr/tmp/$$*" 0 1 2 3 15
31
32 # process the options
33
34 for ARG in "$@"
```

```
35 do
36   case "$ARG" in
37     -e)   CMDL="$CMDL""$ARG "
38           GETPV=0
39           ;;
40     -r*)  ROPT=`echo $ARG | sed 's/..//'`
41           ;;
42     -w*)  WOPT=\'$ARG\'
43           ;;
44     -\?\?)
45           echo $USAGE 1>&2
46           exit $ERET1
47           ;;
48     -*)   CMDL="$CMDL""$ARG "
49           ;;
50     *)    SFILE="$SFILE""$ARG "
51           ;;
52   esac
53 done
54
55 # perform validations checks and set environment
56
57 . /usr/sfm/setsfm
58
59 if [ $GETPV -eq 0 ]
60 then
61
62 # Not allowed to do a get -e if the product version file
63 # is already in use by another user.
64 if [ ! -w "$WDIR/prod/$PROD.pv" -a -f "$SDIR/prod/p.$PROD.pv" ]
65 then
66   echo "ERROR: Product being edited by another user:" 1>&2
67   sact $SDIR/prod/s.$PROD.pv
68   exit $ERET1
69 fi
70
71 # the Product Version File must be a leaf delta, no automatic
72 # branching is allowed. The test transforms the test into a
73 # main trunk versus branch test.
74   if val -r$PSID $SDIR/prod/s.$PROD.pv
75   then
76     TSID=`echo $PSID | sed 's/..$//'`
77     if [ `expr $TSID : '.*'` -eq 1 ]
78     then
79       TSID=`eval $GET -r -g $SDIR/prod/s.$PROD.pv`
80     else
81       TSID=`eval $GET -r$TSID -g $SDIR/prod/s.$PROD.pv`
82     fi
83     if [ "$TSID" != "$PSID" ]
84     then
85       echo "ERROR: Product Version File not current." 1>&2
86       exit $ERET1
87     fi
88   else
89     exit $?
```

```
 90    fi
 91 fi
 92
 93 # The following lines are used to determine the Relative
 94 # Path name (RPATH), which is the path from the WDIR to the
 95 # current working directory.
 96 RPATH=`eval basename \`pwd\``
 97 WPATH=`eval dirname \`pwd\``
 98 until [ "$WDIR" = "$WPATH" -o "$WPATH" = '/' ]
 99 do
100    RPATH=`basename $WPATH`"/$RPATH"
101    WPATH=`dirname $WPATH`
102 done
103 if [ "$WPATH" = '/' ]
104 then
105    echo "ERROR: $WDIR not a valid directory." 1>&2
106    exit $ERET1
107 fi
108
109 # If no source files were specified, retrieve all files
110 # for this component as listed in the Product Version File.
111 if [ -z "$SFILE" ]
112 then
113    CMPNT=`basename $RPATH`
114    SFILE=`eval awk \'\\\\$1 ==\"$CMPNT\" \
115          {printf \"%s \", \\\$2 } \
116          END { printf \"\\\n\" } \' $WDIR/prod/$PROD.pv`
117 fi
118
119 # now execute a get for each SCCS File defined
120 for I in $SFILE
121 do
122
123 # if required, convert to an absolute path name
124    if [ `expr "$I" : '\(.\)'` \\| 'x'` = "/" ]
125    then
126      SPATH=$I
127      SNAME=`basename $I`
128    else
129      SPATH=$SDIR/$RPATH/$I
130      SNAME=$I
131    fi
132
133    echo "$SPATH": 1>&2
134    if val $SPATH
135    then
136      if [ -z "$ROPT" ]
137      then
138        if [ "$SNAME" = "s.$PROD.pv" ]
139        then
140          RSID=-r$PSID
141        else
142          CMPNT=`basename \`dirname $SPATH\``
143          RSID=-r`grep "$CMPNT $SNAME" $WDIR/prod/$PROD.pv\
                   | awk '{print $3}'`
```

```
144        fi
145     else
146        RSID=-r$ROPT
147     fi
148     eval $GET $CMDL $RSID $WOPT $SPATH
149     if [ $? -eq 0 ]
150     then
151        GETOK=0
152     fi
153   fi
154 done
155 if [ ! -w "$WDIR/prod/$PROD.pv" -a $GETPV = 0 -a $GETOK = 0 ]
156 then
157    echo "Getting Product Version File: s.$PROD.pv" 1>&2
158    (CDIR=$WDIR/prod; cd $CDIR; eval $GET -e -r$PSID s.$PROD.pv)
159 fi
```

Discussion

After the command line has been processed (lines 34 through 53), the environmental parameters are set (line 57). The product version file is then checked to see if the **-e** was given on the command line (lines 59 through 91). If the product version file in the current work source tree is not writable and a **p-file** exists in the SCCS source tree, it is assumed that the product is being edited by another user and the command is terminated. Which test to use for determining if the current PSID is a leaf delta depends on whether it is a trunk or branch SID. By stripping off the last two characters (line 76), only R or R.L.B will remain. The test (line 79) for R (the trunk) looks for the mR.mL. The test (line 81) for R.L.B (a branch) looks for R.L.B.mS. If the PSID does not match the retrieved SID, processing is terminated.

Lines 96 through 107 form the standard routine for determining the relative path name. When no file names are entered, lines 111 through 117 are used to extract a list of file names from the product version file.

For each file in the list of files, the routines defined by lines 120 through line 154 are executed. Lines 124 through 131 will, if necessary, convert the file names to an absolute SCCS path name. The next routine performs the actual retrieval of the source file. If the product version file is being retrieved, then the PSID is used as the default SID. For all other files, the default SID is determined by the SID in the product version file.

The last step is to retrieve the product version file if it has not already been retrieved for edit by a previous **(s)get** with the **-e** option.

Name

srmdel   special version of the **rmdel** command.

Syntax

srmdel-r{SID} {SCCS File ...}

Description

In addition to being a preprocessor to the **sfint{xx} -Crmdel** command, the **srmdel** command performs the following functions:

1. If the SID was successfully deleted and the product version file is open for edit, the product version file will be modified. The new SID for the source file will be the leaf SID for the trunk or branch, depending on whether or not the SID deleted was a trunk or branch SID.
2. If a validation program is named in the SCCS file (see discussion of the **v** flag in Chapter 4), an entry is made into the log file. The format is the same as given in Appendix D except that the word "delta" is replaced with "rmdel".

The argument {file . . .} can specify an SCCS file or several SCCS files, or, if no file is specified, all the file names in the current working directory are converted to SCCS file names. The actual path to the SCCS file need not be specified. The **srmdel** command will construct this path from information in the "**.sfmdata**" file.

Options

The option for the **srmdel** command is the same as for the **rmdel** command.

Examples

$ srmdel -r1.5 s.exampl.c

Source

```
1  :
2  # %W% %F% %Y% %D% %Q%
3
4  # srmdel -rmdel command interface
5
6  USAGE="usage: srmdel -r{SID} {SCCS File ...}"
7
8  # Exit Codes and their meanings
9  # 0 - Normal
10 # 1 - Error
11
12 ERET1=1
13
```

```
14 # Temporary file Definitions
15 TMP1=/usr/tmp/$$rmd1
16
17 # Variable Definitions
18 ASID=
19 CDATE=`date '+%D %T'`
20 GET='sfint$PROD -Cget'
21 LFILE=/usr/mradm/logmr
22 PROD=
23 RMDEL='sfint$PROD -Crmdel'
24 RSID=
25 SFILE=
26 STMP=
27 PATH=/bin:/usr/bin:/etc:/usr/sfm
28
29 # Interrupt trap
30 trap "rm -f /usr/tmp/$$*" 0 1 2 3 15
31
32 # process the options
33
34 for ARG  in "$@"
35 do
36    case "$ARG" in
37
38 # for the -r option save the SID to be removed (RSID) and
39 # the ambiguous version (ASID) of the RSID.
40     -r*) RSID=`echo $ARG | sed 's/..//'`
41          ASID=`echo $RSID | sed 's/..$//'`
42          ;;
43     -\?|\?)
44          echo $USAGE 1>&2
45          exit $ERET1
46          ;;
47     *)   SFILE="$SFILE""$ARG "
48          ;;
49    esac
50 done
51
52 # perform validations checks
53
54 . /usr/sfm/setsfm
55 if [ ! -w "$WDIR/prod/$PROD.pv" ]
56 then
57    echo "WARNING: Product Version File cannot be updated." 1>&2
58 fi
59
60 # The following lines are used to determine the Relative
61 # Path (RPATH), which is equal to CDIR - WDIR.
62 RPATH=`eval basename \`pwd\``
63 WPATH=`eval dirname \`pwd\``
64 until [ "$WDIR" = "$WPATH" -o "$WPATH" = '/' ]
65 do
66    RPATH=`basename $WPATH`"/$RPATH"
67    WPATH=`dirname $WPATH`
68 done
```

```
69 if [ "$WPATH" = '/' ]
70 then
71   echo "ERROR: $WDIR not a valid directory." 1>&2
72   exit $ERET1
73 fi
74
75 # if no file specified, apply to all files in current
76 # working directory
77 if [ -z "$SFILE" ]
78 then
79   cd $CDIR
80   for I in *
81   do
82     SFILE="$SFILE""s.$I "
83   done
84 fi
85
86 # now execute an rmdel for each SCCS File defined
87
88 for I in $SFILE
89 do
90
91   # if necessary, convert to absolute SCCS Path Name
92   if [ `expr "$I" : '\(.\)'` \| 'x'` = "/" ]
93   then
94     SPATH=$I
95   else
96     SPATH=$SDIR/$RPATH/$I
97   fi
98
99   # if a valid SCCS File, remove the delta
100   echo "$SPATH: \c"
101   if val -s $SPATH
102   then
103     SNAME=`basename $SPATH`
104     eval $RMDEL -r$RSID $SPATH 2> $TMP1
105     if [ $? = 0 -a -w "$WDIR/prod/$PROD.pv" -a $SNAME != "s.$PROD.pv" ]
106     then
107       echo "deleted."
108
109       # If everything is ok, then update the Product Version File
110       CMPNT=`eval basename \`dirname $SPATH\``
111       TSID=`eval $GET -r$ASID -g $SPATH`
112       ed -s $WDIR/prod/$PROD.pv <<-EOF
113         /$CMPNT $SNAME/c
114         $CMPNT $SNAME $TSID
115         .
116         w
117         q
118         EOF
119
120 # if there is a validation program, make a note in the log file
121       MPGM=`prs -d:MP: $SPATH`
122       if [ -n "$MPGM" ]
123       then
```

```
124           STMP=`echo $SNAME | sed 's/..//'`
125           prs -r$RSID -a -d:MR: $SPATH > $TMP1
126           exec 3< $TMP1
127           exec 4<&0
128           exec 0<&3
129           while read MRNUM
130           do
131             if [ -n "$MRNUM" ]
132             then
133               echo "rmdel $STMP $MRNUM $CDATE" >> $LFILE
134             fi
135         done
136           exec 0<&4
137        fi
138     else
139      echo "failed."
140       cat $TMP1
141       fi
142    else
143        echo "$SPATH: Not a valid SCCS File"
144    fi
145 done
```

Discussion

In addition to the validation checks performed by **setsfm**, the product version file is checked to see if it is writable (lines 55 through 57).

The standard relative path name routine is defined in lines 60 through 73. If no files are specified, a list of SCCS file names is created based on the file names in the current working directory (lines 77 through 84).

Lines 88 through 145 are repeated for every file in the defined list. If necessary, the SCCS path is added to the SCCS file name (lines 92 through 97). If the file name is a valid SCCS file (line 101), the delta is removed in line 104. Lines 109 through 118 define the routine for updating the product version file with the new SID. If a validation program has been defined, Lines 121 through 136 define the routine for adding an entry to the log file defined in line 21.

Name

      sunget   Special version of the **unget** command.

Syntax

      sunget [unget command options] {SCCS File . . .}

Description

The **sunget** command is a preprocessor to the **sfint{xx} -Cunget** command. However, the **-n** option for **sunget**, (see options below) is handled differently than the same option of the **unget** command.

The argument {file . . .} can specify an SCCS file or several SCCS files, or, if no file is specified, all the file names in the current working directory are converted to SCCS file names. The actual path to the SCCS file need not be specified. The **sunget** command will construct this path from information in the ".sfmdata" file.

Options

The options for the **sunget** command are the same as for the **unget** command. However, the **-n** option has a change in its syntax. The **sunget** command will retrieve a new version of the file based on the retrieved SID specified in the p-file.

Examples

$ sget -n s.exampl.c

Source

```
 1 :
 2 # %W% %F% %Y% %D% %Q%
 3
 4 # sunget -unget command interface
 5
 6 USAGE="usage: sunget [unget command options] {SCCS File ...}"
 7
 8 # Exit Codes and their meanings
 9 # 0 - Normal
10 # 1 - Error
11
12 ERET1=1
13
14 # Temporary file Definitions
15 TMP1=/usr/tmp/$$ugt1
16 TMP2=/usr/tmp/$$ugt2
17
18 # Variable Definitions
19 CMDL=
20 GET='sfint$PROD -Cget'
21 PROD=
22 SFILE=
23 STMP=
```

```
24 KEEP=1
25 PATH=/bin:/usr/bin:/etc:/usr/sfm
26 UNGET='sfint$PROD -Cunget'
27
28 # Interrupt trap
29 trap "rm -f /usr/tmp$$*" 0 1 2 3 15
30
31 # process the options
32
33 for ARG in "$@"
34 do
35   case "$ARG" in
36     -n) KEEP=0
37         ;;
38     -\?|\?)
39         echo $USAGE 1>&2
40         exit $ERET1
41         ;;
42     -*) CMDL="$CMDL""$ARG "
43         ;;
44     *)  SFILE="$SFILE""$ARG "
45         ;;
46   esac
47 done
48
49 # perform validations checks
50
51 . /usr/sfm/setsfm
52
53 # The following lines are used to determine the Relative
54 # Path (RPATH). The RPATH is equal to the CDIR - WDIR.
55 RPATH=`eval basename \`pwd\``
56 WPATH=`eval dirname \`pwd\``
57 until [ "$WDIR" = "$WPATH" -o "$WPATH" = '/' ]
58 do
59  RPATH=`basename $WPATH`"/$RPATH"
60  WPATH=`dirname $WPATH`
61 done
62 if [ "$WPATH" = '/' ]
63 then
64   echo "ERROR: $WDIR not a valid directory." 1>&2
65   exit $ERET1
66 fi
67
68 # If no files are specified, set the list to all files in
69 # the current directory.
70 if [ -z "$SFILE" ]
71 then
72   cd $CDIR
73   for I in *
74   do
75     SFILE="$SFILE"" s."$I
76   done
77 fi
78
```

```
79 # now execute an unget for each SCCS File defined
80
81 for I in $SFILE
82 do
83
84 # if necessary, convert file names to an absolute path
85 if [ `expr "$I" : '\(.\)'\\| 'x'` = "/" ]
86    then
87      SNAME=$I
88    else
89      SNAME=$SDIR/$RPATH/$I
90    fi
91
92    # unget the file if it is a valid SCCS file
93    echo "$SNAME":
94    if val -s $SNAME
95    then
96      sact $SNAME 1> $TMP1 2> /dev/null
97      eval $UNGET $CMDL $SNAME > $TMP2
98
99      # If unget successful and -n flag given, retrieve the version
100     # from which the get was based.
101     if [ $? = 0 -a $KEEP -eq 0 ]
102     then
103       DSID=`sed 1q $TMP2`
104       echo $DSID
105       NSID=`grep "$DSID" $TMP1 | awk '{print $1}'`
106       eval $GET -r$NSID -s $SNAME
107
108     # else report the results of the unget
109     else
110       cat $TMP2 | sed 1q
111     fi
112   else
113     echo "$SNAME: Not a valid SCCS File"
114   fi
115 done
```

Discussion

The standard validation routine, **setsfm**, is performed in line 51. It is followed by the standard routine for determining the relative path name (lines 59 through 66). If no file names were entered, a list of SCCS file names is created for each file in the current working directory in lines 70 through 77.

Lines 81 through 115 are repeated for each SCCS file specified. If necessary, the SCCS path is added to the file name (lines 85 through 90). If the file is a valid SCCS file, the contents of the **p-file** are saved (line 96) and then the **unget** command is executed (line 97). If the unget was successful and the file is to be kept, the SID is derived from the **p-file** (lines 103 through 105) and a new copy is retrieved (line 106).

Note: The filtering of the output through **sed** in lines 103 and 110 is a result of a bug in the **unget** command. In System V/386, Release 3.0, the **unget** command would print the SID twice on the standard output if it were directed into a pipe or a file. This anomaly may or may not be present in other versions of the command.

Name

verst   Verify product version file.

Syntax

verst [-u]

Description

The purpose of this shell script is to verify the accuracy of the work source tree. The PSID is verified to ensure that it is a leaf delta. If the PSID is valid, then the SID of the product version file (as defined in the what string) is checked to make sure that it matches the PSID. If the product version file is open for editing, the **p-file** is checked. If the product version file is not a leaf delta and it is not open for editing, the correct version of the product version file is retrieved.

The **verst** command then verifies that each source file listed in the product version file follows the rule of being either **mR.mL** or **R.L.B.mS**. This follows from the premise that, when the product version file is the leaf delta of the trunk or any branch, the SID for each source file listed in the product version file should also be a leaf delta. If it is not, then either a new product is under development, the product version file is from a branch that is not current with changes made to the trunk, or there is an potential error in the product version file. When the SID for a source file is not a leaf delta, a message is printed on standard output. If the **-u** option was given, the user is asked if the error should be corrected. If the answer is positive, the product version file is modified and the correct delta is retrieved.

The **verst** command also issues a message for any source file that it does not find in the product version file. As a final step, all source files that are in the product version file but not in the work source tree are listed.

Options

   -u When this option is present, if any discrepancy between the SID of the source file and the retrieved SID is found, the option to correct the error is given.

Examples

$ verst
$ verst -u

Source

```
1  :
2  # %W% %F% %Y% %D% %Q%
3
4  # verst - Verify Product Version File
5
6  USAGE="\
7  usage: verst [-u]"
8
9  # Exit Codes and their meanings
10 # 0 - Normal
11 # 1 - Error
12
13 ERET1=1
14
15 # Temporary file Definitions
16 TMP1=/usr/tmp/$$dst1
17 TMP2=/usr/tmp/$$dst2
18 TMP3=/usr/tmp/$$dst3
19
20 # Variable Definitions
21 GET='sfint$PROD -Cget'
22 UPDATE=1
23 PATH=/bin:/usr/bin:/etc:/usr/sfm
24
25 # Interrupt trap
26 trap "rm -f /usr/tmp/$$*" 0 1 2 3 15
27
28 # process options
29
30 for ARG in "$@"
31 do
32   case "$ARG" in
33     -u)   UPDATE=0
34           ;;
35    -\?|\?|*)
36           echo "$USAGE" 1>&2
37           exit $ERET1
38           ;;
39   esac
40 done
41
42 # perform validation checks and set environment
43
44 . /usr/sfm/setsfm
45
46 if [ ! -f "$WDIR/prod/$PROD.pv" ]
47 then
```

```
48    echo "ERROR: Cannot find Product Version file." 1>&2
49    exit $ERET1
50 fi
51
52 # Check if PSID is a leaf delta
53
54 if val -r$PSID $SDIR/prod/s.$PROD.pv
55 then
56
57    # leaf SID for trunk or branch
58    TSID=`echo $PSID | sed 's/..$//'`
59    if [ `expr $TSID : '.*'` -eq 1 ]
60    then
61      TSID=`eval $GET -r -g $SDIR/prod/s.$PROD.pv`
62    else
63      TSID=`eval $GET -r$TSID -g $SDIR/prod/s.$PROD.pv`
64    fi
65
66    # compare against PSID
67    if [ "$TSID" != "$PSID" ]
68    then
69      echo "Product SID ($PSID) not a leaf delta."
70      echo "PSID in .sfmdata is incorrect - change [ y or n ]? "\\c
71      while read ANS
72      do
73        case $ANS in
74          y*|Y*) echo "Changing PSID to $TSID."
75                 sed /PSID/s/$PSID/$TSID/ < $WDIR/.sfmdata > $TMP1
76                 cp $TMP1 $WDIR/.sfmdata
77                 PSID=$TSID
78                 break
79                 ;;
80          n*|N*) if [ $UPDATE -eq 0 ]
81                 then
82                    echo "Update (-n) Option ignored. Only leaf delta"
83                    echo "can be updated."
84                    UPDATE=1
85                 fi
86                 break
87                 ;;
88          *)     echo "Please enter [ y or n ]? "\\c
89                 ;;
90        esac
91      done
92    fi
93 else
94    exit $?
95 fi
96
97 # Check the SID of the Product Version File
98 # Note, the following test for TSID depends on
99 # using the standard what string.
100
101 if [ ! -w $WDIR/prod/$PROD.pv ]
102 then
```

```
103    TSID=`what $WDIR/prod/$PROD.pv | tail -1 | awk '{print $2}'`
104    if [ "$TSID" != "$PSID" ]
105    then
106      echo "Product SID ($PSID) does not match SID of $PROD.pv" 1>&2
107      echo "Will get correct Product Version File." 1>&2
108      (CDIR=$WDIR/prod; cd $CDIR; \
109      eval $GET -r$PSID -s $SDIR/prod/s.$PROD.pv)
110    fi
111 fi
112
113 if [ ! -w $WDIR/prod/$PROD.pv -a $UPDATE -eq 0 ]
114 then
115   echo "Getting $SDIR/prod/s.$PROD.pv for -u option" 1>&2
116   (CDIR=$WDIR/prod; cd $CDIR; \
117   eval $GET -r$PSID -e $SDIR/prod/s.$PROD.pv)
118 fi
119
120 # Check the files against the product version file
121
122 (CDIR=$WDIR; cd $CDIR; \
123 find . -type f ! -name $PROD.pv ! -name .sfmdata -print > $TMP2)
124 sort $TMP2 > $TMP1
125 exec 3< $TMP1
126 exec 4<&0
127 exec 0<&3
128 while read WPATH
129 do
130    WFILE=`basename $WPATH`
131    SFILE="s.$WFILE"
132    PFILE="p.$WFILE"
133    CMPNT=`basename \`dirname $WPATH\``
134    RPATH=`echo \`dirname $WPATH\` | sed 's/..//'`
135
136    # Is there a matching SCCS File
137    if [ ! -f $SDIR/$RPATH/$SFILE ]
138    then
139      echo "Cannot find SCCS File: $SDIR/$RPATH/$SFILE" 1>&2
140      continue
141    fi
142
143    # Does it exist in the Product Version File
144    if (grep "$CMPNT $SFILE" $WDIR/prod/$PROD.pv > $TMP2)
145    then
146      PVSID=`awk '{print $3}' $TMP2`
147      cat $TMP2 >> $TMP3
148    else
149      echo "Cannot find $CMPNT $SFILE in Product Version File." 1>&2
150      continue
151    fi
152
153    # Is the SID in the Product Version File Valid
154    if val -r$PVSID -s $SDIR/$RPATH/$SFILE
155    then
156      true
157    else
```

```
158        echo "$CMPNT $WFILE $PVSID - SID is invalid or bad SCCS file."
159        continue
160    fi
161
162    # Is the SID of the source file a Leaf Delta
163    TSID=`echo $PVSID | sed 's/..$//'`
164    if [ `expr $TSID : '.*'` -eq 1 ]
165    then
166      TSID=`eval $GET -r -g $SDIR/$RPATH/$SFILE`
167    else
168      TSID=`eval $GET -r$TSID -g $SDIR/$RPATH/$SFILE`
169    fi
170    if [ "$TSID" != "$PVSID" ]
171    then
172
173      # if file is being edited, then check p-file
174      # this may be a new branch from an older delta
175      if [ -f $SDIR/$RPATH/$PFILE -a -w $WDIR/$RPATH/$WFILE ]
176      then
177        if `grep "$PVSID" $SDIR/$RPATH/$PFILE > /dev/null 2>&1`
178        then
179          echo "$CMPNT $WFILE open for edit - assumed OK."
180          sact $SDIR/$RPATH/$SFILE
181        else
182          echo "$CMPNT $WFILE open for edit - needs to be checked."
183          sact $SDIR/$RPATH/$SFILE
184        fi
185
186    # else find if correct version is to be retrieved
187    else
188      echo "$CMPNT $WFILE $PVSID not a leaf delta."
189      if [ $UPDATE -eq 0 ]
190      then
191        exec 0<&4
192        echo "Correct the problem [ y or n ]? "\\c
193        while read ANS
194        do
195          case $ANS in
196            y*|Y*) ed -s $WDIR/prod/$PROD.pv <<-EOF
197                      /$CMPNT $SFILE/c
198                      $CMPNT $SFILE $TSID
199                      .
200                      w
201                      q
202                      EOF
203                   PVSID=$TSID
204                   break
205                   ;;
206            n*|N*)   break
207                   ;;
208            *)       echo "Please enter [ y or n ]? "\\c
209                   ;;
210          esac
211        done
212        exec 0<&3
```

```
213        fi
214      fi
215    fi
216
217    # if the file is not being edited, check to verify that it
218    # is the correct version. Again, this assumes that the
219    # standard ID Keyword string is being used.
220    if [ ! -w $WDIR/$RPATH/$WFILE ]
221    then
222      TSID=`what $WDIR/$RPATH/$WFILE | sed -n 2p | awk '{print $2}'`
223      if [ "$TSID" != "$PVSID" ]
224      then
225        echo "$CMPNT $WFILE $PVSID does not match SID of file." 1>&2
226        echo "Will get correct version of $WFILE." 1>&2
227        (CDIR=$WDIR/$RPATH; cd $CDIR; \
228          eval $GET -r$PVSID $SDIR/$RPATH/$SFILE)
229      fi
230    fi
231 done
232
233 # Once the files have been verified, check to see if any files
234 # defined in the Product Version File are missing.
235 sed 1d < $WDIR/prod/$PROD.pv | diff $TMP3 - > $TMP1
236 if [ -s $TMP1 ]
237 then
238 echo "Warning: The following were not found in the\
        Work Source Tree." 1>&2
239 cat $TMP1 1<&2
240 fi
241 echo "Version check complete." 1>&2
```

Discussion

This is a large script composed of several major elements. All environmental variables are validated by the **setsfm** script described in this appendix. The first major test (lines 52 through 95) is to verify that the PSID is a leaf delta. If it is not, then the user has the option of updating the **.sfmdata** file with the correct SID or not. The resulting PSID is then checked against the retrieved product version file. Unless the Product Version is writable (open for edit), the PSID is assumed to represent the correct SID and, if necessary, a new copy of the product version file will be retrieved (lines 101 through 111).

If the product version file has not been retrieved for edit and if the **-u** option has been given, the product version file is retrieved for edit in lines 113 through 118.

In lines 122 through 124, a list is made of all the files in the work source tree (except the product version file and the .sfmdata file). In lines 125 through 231, this list is cross checked to the product version file, the corresponding SCCS file, and the source file. Any discrepancies are noted and, if the **-u** option was given, the leaf delta for a source file can be retrieved.

In line 147, a list is made of every source file for which there is a match in the product version file. In lines 235 through 240, the above list is compared against the product version file. The differences, consisting of those files that were in the product version file but not found in the work source tree, are printed on the standard error.

Note: All work files and executable files that are the result of building a product will be reported as errors since there are no corresponding SCCS files. To avoid listing these files as errors, the work source tree should be cleared of all these files.

Glossary

ambiguous SID—When only one or three components of a SID are given, it is called an ambiguous SID. When only the Release is specified, most SCCS commands will take this to mean **R.mL**, which is the maximum Level currently assigned. The same applies when three components are given. The **R.L.B** is taken to mean **R.L.B.mS**.

application text file—A form of **text file** created and modified by the user of a system for application purposes, as opposed to special system files such as /etc/passwd.

child source file—The resulting source file after modifications have been made to its **parent source file**.

component—A stand-alone building block that is combined with other components to form a product. As a part of the source tree, a component is a directory that may consist of source files and/or subcomponents.

d-file—A temporary file created by the **delta** command. It is identical to the **g-file** before any changes were made and is used in determining what changes were made.

data keywords—The variables used by the **prs** command to identify all the elements of an SCCS file.

delta—Refers to the differences between two versions of a file. Thus, a delta file is a file containing the differences between two other files. Under SCCS, all deltas are combined into a single file. A delta is identified by its **SID**. Since SCCS reconstructs a source file starting from a particular **SID**, a delta also refers to a particular version of a source file.

delta sequence number—A number used internally by SCCS to identify each delta. As the name implies, it is a sequential number given to each delta.

delta SID—The SID of the delta to be created as defined in the **p-file**. To prevent the creation of duplicate SIDs, the delta SID is determined when the **get -e** is executed.

development machine—The machine on which the work source tree is maintained. It is connected to the source library machine by some mode of communications, such as UUCP or a local area network.

dynamic application text file—An **application text file** that undergoes periodic cycles of modification such that there are different versions of the file.

effective user—First, read the definition for **real user**. In most cases, the real user and effective user are the same. However, they can be different. If the SUID bit of the command to be executed is set, then the effective user is the owner of the command. When this happens, the real user inherits the permissions of the owner of the command. Thus, the user that affects the permissions is the owner of the command and not the real user.

g-file—The retrieved source file that is created in the current working directory and is owned by the real user. The name of the file is created by removing the "s." from the SCCS file name.

id keywords—A group of variables that can be inserted into a source file. These variables can be used to identify the SCCS origin of the source file.

l-file—A file created by the **-l** option of the **get** command. It provides the details as to which deltas where combined to create the source file.

p-file—A temporary file created by the **get** command to indicate that a source file has been retrieved for editing. The information in this file is used by the **delta** command when creating the delta entry in the delta table. A record is created for each delta SID. This record is removed when the delta is made. If the **p-file** contains no other records, it is deleted by the **delta** command.

parent source file—The source file that is the starting point for modifications to a particular version.

product—Refers to a complete software system, software package, or document. For example, a general ledger package, a 'C' compiler, or the source file management tools defined in this book would be called products.

product class—A group of products that share common source files. For example, general ledger, accounts payable, and accounts receivable would form a product class if they shared common source files.

product version file—A special file that is used to identify the SID for all the source files that are part of a product. The data elements contained in the file are the component name, SCCS file name, and SID.

progeny—The descendants of any **parent source file**.

q-file—A temporary copy of the **p-file** created during the execution of a **delta** command. The reason for the **q-file** is the same as for the **x-file**.

real user—In /etc/passwd, every login name has an associated number called the user identification (UID). When a user executes a command, a process is started. The process identifies the user who executed the process by the real UID.

SCCS control character—An SOH (control-A) character used to identify the following line as an SCCS control record (see Section 3.5). As a result, records in the source file cannot begin with an SOH character.

SCCS source tree—The source tree for a product, which consists of components, subcomponents, and SCCS files.

SID—Abbreviation for SCCS identification string. Every delta in an SCCS file is identified by a SID, which becomes the name of the delta. A SID can have up to four components which are the release, level, branch, and sequence numbers. Every delta on the trunk of an SCCS file is identified by two components: **R.L**. Every delta on a branch is identified by four components: **R.L.B.S**.

source file—A common term for the **dynamic application text file**. Although the name derives from their being used as source code files, source files may also be used for documentation.

source library machine—Refers to the computer on which the SCCS source tree for all products is maintained.

subcomponents—A directory residing under a component or another subcomponent directory that may contain source files and/or subcomponents.

text file—A file that contains primarily alphanumeric characters. Occasionally, a text file may contain some special characters used for controlling output format.

version control—The ability to maintain and track different versions of a source file or product using either manual or automated systems.

work source tree—A mirror image of the **SCCS source tree** in which the SCCS files have been replaced by source files for a particular version of the **product**.

x-file—A temporary copy of the SCCS file being updated. It is created as insurance against file damage caused by abnormal termination of the update. The name of the file is created by substituting the "s." of the SCCS file name with "x.". When processing is complete, the SCCS file is removed and the **x-file** is renamed to be the SCCS file.

z-file—A temporary file created by SCCS commands during the modification of an SCCS file. This file is used to prevent any other SCCS commands from attempting to modify the SCCS file at the same time. The name is created by substituting the "s." of the SCCS file name with "z.". When processing is complete, the file is removed.

Index

A

.sfmdata file, 136, 166, 169, 173, 177,
    184–86, 190, 195, 199, 207
admin command, 13–14, 30, 33–44, 46,
    60, 62, 73–78, 86, 119, 121, 128,
    134–35, 160, 164, 172
  -a option, 37, 74
  -d option, 75–76
  -e option, 74
  -f option, 39, 75
  -h option, 89, 102
  -i option, 14, 35–36
  -m option, 37
  -n option, 14, 34–35
  -r option, 36, 40
  -t option, 43, 78
  -y option, 36
  -z option, 88
Ambiguous SID, 48, 53, 80, 95, 101–2,
    104–5
  R, 49, 61
  R.L.B., 50, 52, 77
ar command, 23
Arguments, 13

B

bdiff command, 67, 70, 102
Branch delta, 24, 26, 40, 50, 52–53, 64,
    77, 85, 124, 148
Branches, 2–5, 8–9, 24–25, 40–41, 46,
    48, 50, 53–54, 61, 63–64, 75, 77,
    85–87, 96, 105–6, 122–23, 125,
    134–37, 144, 147–48

C

cdc command, 62, 79, 119, 159
  -m option, 80–81
  -r option, 80
  -y option, 80–81
Chief programmer teams, 6, 144
Command format, 13
Command option, 13
comb command, 51, 79, 82–86, 119, 135
  -c option, 85–86
  -o option, 85–86
  -p option, 84–86
  -s option, 83, 86